PATHS TO RENEWAL

Given to the Carmel in Concord,
MA —
      January 23, 2004

Rev. Zachary Grant, ofm Cap.

— Take and read !

At the close of the twentieth century, as we prepare to embark on a new millennium, we are more and more aware of the fact that "*our difficult age has a special need of prayer*. In the course of history — both in the past and in the present — many men and women have borne witness to the importance of prayer by consecrating themselves to the *praise of God* and to the *life of prayer*, especially in monasteries and convents; so too recent years have been seeing a growth in the number of people who, in ever more widespread movements and groups, are giving first place to prayer and seeking in prayer a *renewal* of their spiritual life" (*Dominum et vivificantem*, 65).

Paths to Renewal

The Spiritualities of Six Religious Founders

Augustine of Hippo
Benedict of Nursia
Dominic Guzman
Francis of Assisi
Ignatius of Loyola
Teresa of Avila

ZACHARY GRANT, OFM CAP

Foreword by
John Cardinal O'Connor
Archbishop of New York

ALBA·HOUSE   NEW·YORK
SOCIETY OF ST. PAUL, 2187 VICTORY BLVD., STATEN ISLAND, NEW YORK 10314

ST PAULS

Library of Congress Cataloging-in-Publication Data

Grant, Zachary.
    Paths to renewal: the spiritualities of six religious founders:
Augustine of Hippo, Benedict of Nursia, Dominic Guzman,
Francis of Assisi, Ignatius of Loyola, Teresa of Avila / Zachary Grant.
        p.   cm.
    ISBN 0-8189-0794-0
    1. Monastic and religious life. 2. Monasticism and religious
orders. 3. Spiritual life — Catholic Church. 4. Catholic Church —
Doctrines.   I. Title.
    BX2435.G73   1998
    255—dc21   97-18268
                                                 CIP

Produced and designed in the United States of America by the
Fathers and Brothers of the Society of St. Paul,
2187 Victory Boulevard, Staten Island, New York 10314,
as part of their communications apostolate.

ISBN: 0-8189-0794-0

Printing Information:

Current Printing - first digit   1   2   3   4   5   6   7   8   9   10

Year of Current Printing - first year shown

1998   1999   2000   2001   2002   2003   2004   2005

DEDICATED TO

The Beloved People of St. Michael Parish
East New York, Brooklyn
on whose time this book was written.

CONTENTS

ACKNOWLEDGMENTS

A special word of thanks must go to John Cardinal O'Connor, Archbishop of New York, for graciously consenting to write the Foreword for this book.

I am deeply grateful to those from the several spirituality traditions who have reviewed the text for accuracy of content and offered valuable suggestions.

Paschal Baumstein, OSB
Belmont, NC

Arthur Bender, SJ
New York, NY

Justin Biase, OFM Conv.
Staten Island, NY

Michael Griffin, OCD
Holy Hill, WI

Thomas McKenna, CM
Jamaica, NY

John E. Rotelle, OSA
Villanova, PA

Urban Voll, OP
New York, NY

I want also to thank those who read the manuscript, made some suggestions, and assured me that the book would be welcomed *by the laity as well as clergy and religious.* These include Matthew and Leticia Cole (Hendersonville, NC), Sr. James Margaret Farrell, SSJ (Springfield, MA), Cecilia Grant (Brooklyn, NY), Kenneth and Anne Walsh (Levittown, NY).

FOREWORD

John Cardinal O'Connor

"Is your name Jesus?" Father Zachary tells us it was many years ago that a child asked him that question. It's the question asked of John the Baptist almost 2,000 years ago. "Are you the Christ, or are we to look for another?" It is a haunting question, a disturbing question, a question every Christian must ask of himself or herself in only slightly modified form. "Is my demeanor, is my behavior such that I could be mistaken for Jesus?"

It would not be far off the mark to suggest that *Paths to Renewal* is, more than anything else, a search among the six great religious orders to find the answer to that question in yet another form: "Does Jesus live here?" For Father Zachary, the answer to this latter question seems to serve as an index, or even a determinant, of whether or not a particular religious life is authentic. Each of the six great religious figures he cites soon or late had to root his or her search in the Person of Christ and to try to determine how closely he or she approximated the Image of Jesus in living out the religious life.

Even the Church herself, the author insists, must be seen as Jesus. For me this is a crucial insight. None of the six great religious orders has any meaning or relevancy outside the Church. If the Church is, indeed, the Body of Christ, unless a religious order is a vital, vibrant, dynamic, functioning member of that Body it is not only lifeless in itself, but life-destroying for its own members.

As a President of the 1994 Synod on Consecrated Life, it

was my privilege to listen to some 260 papers presented by bishops and religious in the general assemblies of the Synod. Moreover, I sat in on many of the informal small group discussions outside the Synod hall. Some I attended were in English, some in Italian. Most striking to me throughout all proceedings was the keen awareness that all the representatives of consecrated life present from all over the world, despite linguistic, cultural, ethnic, racial, or other differences were members of the one Church, the one Body of Christ. And I found myself looking for correlations between papers presented and discussions pursued and clearly apparent vital membership in that one Body. Perhaps it was only my perception, but it seemed to me that the more vibrantly a paper read or a word spoken resonated with the Church, the more alive, the healthier, did the particular form of religious life seem to be.

In August of 1993 a magnificent World Day of Youth took place in Denver, Colorado, presided over by Pope John Paul II. The vitality of his presence and his obvious love for the hundreds of thousands of young people from 70 different countries was magical. Then Irish woman singer Dana appeared on the huge stage where the Holy Father was sitting, and began to sing, "We are one Body, one Body in Christ." The effect was instant and electric. Hundreds of thousands of young strangers grasped one another's hand and joined in her singing, tears running down their cheeks. I spoke with many of them later. All told me the same thing: they had never before experienced such solidarity in being Catholic; never before had they been so invigorated by the realization that they were all members of the same Body of Christ. And there was his Vicar on earth, the living sign of unity, sitting on the stage.

Both my reflection on the Synod and the remembrance of Denver may seem far afield from Father Zachary's theme. I believe, on the contrary, that each is but an excursion into his theme as experienced in two unique, dramatically different situations: dramatically different except for the extraordinary fact that the Pope presided over both, personally present to all in each case.

I wish I had had *Paths to Renewal* during the years of my own seminary formation and throughout my priesthood. I will at least have it in my final years as a bishop. And I will have it for my own community, the Sisters of Life, who are trying so hard to be holy and to merit the question asked of Father Zachary so many years ago: "Is your name Jesus?" Indeed, if I myself try hard enough now to live as any one of the six great religious he describes, perhaps one day the question will even be asked of me. How wondrous that would be.

May 30, 1997

PROLOGUE

This book was written for two reasons. I felt a need to do something special in the final years of my allotted three score and ten, which I am fast completing. The work will also serve to ease my conscience. For many years now thoughts expressed here have been used in various talks and sermons that I have given. Good people have suggested that I put them in writing to help those who give spiritual direction. Now I have completed what might have been done many years ago. My decision to make a start came in a burst of inspiration on July 15, 1994. My sister Mary, just a year older than I, had died suddenly the previous month. That she died on my birthday made me a bit more pensive. She had seemed in good health, as was I. Perhaps, my thoughts ran, I do not have that much time left either.

That summer afternoon in 1994 I was on a private retreat at Mount Savior Benedictine Abbey in Pine City, New York, and sat reading in a small library at the guest house. The sudden roar of a powerful engine made me think that a helicopter was about to land on the lawn just outside the building. Not so. Rather, someone was shattering the monastic silence with an old power mower which he was riding back and forth over the vast expanse of green which encircled the monastery chapel. The noise seemed sacrilegious in such a place, and even more so as it continued for about forty minutes.

When quiet returned, so did my reasoning. If the abbey was to have a lawn so large — and it certainly contributed to a sense of solitude and distance from commercial bustle — then an occasional intrusion of modern life was acceptable. A monk working a hand mower would need many hours in the spring and summer to keep the hilly land beautiful for the glory of God and as an aid to contemplation. And there is other work to be done, much more essential, and monks need time to pray, which is their vocation. Saint Benedict might have tolerated machine noise even at Monte Cassino if it would allow the monks to be more faithful to choir, day and night.

I had come on retreat to this monastic place from active parochial ministry because of a strong awareness that I must "go apart to a quiet place" now and then, as Jesus did, to be true to my priestly and Franciscan vocation. I am not a monk, but the monks provided me that place apart. Francis of Assisi had his Carceri. The modern Franciscan, especially a parish priest, must often find his own place.

A broader dilemma faces all religious today, who are cultural generations and centuries away from the concrete example of their founders. How should we respond, as servants of the Church, to the needs of God's people in the manner and with the special charism that makes us different? Do we not contribute to the life of the Church as no others can? Can we be faithful to a spirituality that first surfaced during a different era in a form which cannot realistically be replicated today?

Yet, if the principles of a particular spirituality are valid, indeed the work of the Holy Spirit, then it is imperative to find the way that such a spirit is best made incarnate in the Church today. Our religious congregations do not just preserve the memories of their founders. We demonstrate that their example has validity now as in a bygone age. The ultimate test of their modern viability is how well they influence the spiritual lives of the laity, who in this generation more than ever have been called to holiness and apostolic commitment in secular society.

With this book I wish to add my voice to the dialogue. I evaluate and compare six fundamentally distinct spirituality traditions which are the legacies of six very unique saints. They have contributed to the vitality of the Church as no others have done — and do so long after their earthly sojourn. The spiritual doctrines which they taught by word and example are still embodied in the religious communities which the Holy Spirit, through them, brought into being at some very critical times in the Church's history.

I speak of Augustine and Benedict for the troublesome age following the fall of the Roman Empire and the legalization of Christianity; of Dominic and Francis when the society of the Middle Ages was heading toward the disintegration of the feudal system to which the Church structures were bonded; of Ignatius and Teresa in the very confusing post-reformation period. These were pivotal times when the Church needed to move in new directions.

In every century new congregations of religious have flourished and produced remarkable men and women who have given new insights into the spiritual life. Looking forward from the sixteenth century, we can think immediately of Angela Merici, Francis de Sales, Frances de Chantal, Vincent de Paul, John Eudes, John Baptist de la Salle, Louis Marie Grignion de Montfort, Alphonsus Liguori, Paul of the Cross, and Don Bosco. Yet I have limited myself to the *Great Six*. I feel that all other orders, reforms and movements (and the holy persons associated with them) have indeed produced important developments to the basic six themes. They molded the established spirituality traditions into new forms that were faith-responses to the circumstances and needs of the Church in their respective generations.

The common opinion would support this view. Even casual observers of religious life have heard about Carmelites and Benedictines; and can appreciate the humor of a story that begins: "Once there was a Dominican, and a Franciscan, and a Jesuit studying in the same room when the light went out...!" Of course, the whole world has heard about *The Confessions of Saint Augustine*.

As all religious must, I have had to look at my own

Franciscan way of life and try to understand it in the modern context. I consider it a very distinct and unique way that is understood better when contrasted with the other five. I keep in mind that all share the essential foundations of the Christian life, follow the same Gospel, practice the same virtues, make use of the same Sacraments, and that we are all united in the Church established by Jesus, the Son of.God. That Church which we serve gives us all our validity. Also I try to remember that no spirituality is inherently better than the rest. The Franciscan way is only best for me.

This book is the result of my often unscholarly attempt to comprehend how Saint Francis differed from the others, how the others differed among themselves, and how these differences are reflected in the lives of their disciples today. My efforts might be of help to anyone who is concerned with the renewal of religious life as called for by the Second Vatican Council. We have been challenged to return to the spirit of our founders and bring that spirit to the current needs of the People of God. The Church will not be served if we allow ourselves to be haunted by the specter of spiritual relativism which allows for no concrete distinctions. Our differences must not be seen as cosmetic.

Hence, we begin with the premise that Augustine, Benedict, Dominic, Francis, Ignatius, and Teresa gave us very distinct spiritualities that are valid today, even if the distinctions are without the sharpness of former ages. They were each influenced by different ecclesiastical realities, and each lived in a very special time and place. Their respective responses to the needs of the Church in their day differed from each other very dramatically. Others who came after them developed new variances and differing emphases within these traditions. This is a key consideration. The Church's needs are complex, yet complementary. There is not one solution that fits all problems.

Of utmost importance is what the laity and secular clergy expect of religious, to whom they look for signs of the kingdom of heaven. The spirituality traditions of which we speak affect *every* Catholic, clergy and laity alike, because they are the patrimony of the entire Church. Hence, all of us are helped by properly understanding the origin and intent of the tradition that is the impetus of our personal spiritual journey. To those who are looking for their distinct role as lay persons in this Vatican II era, and to those religious who are intent on seeing that the laity take their proper place in Church renewal, this book will be useful. Reform, both ecclesial and personal, must be joined to holiness of life.

I have the hope that others will be inspired to carry the study deeper and broader, with more solid scholarship, and with very specific and concrete applications. Love for the Church, and for Jesus whom we follow, demands our every effort.

Zachary Grant, OFM Cap

CHAPTER ONE

THE GREAT SIX — WHENCE THEY CAME

I n order to begin our evaluation and comparison of the *Great Six*, and their unique contributions to the spiritual life and holiness of the Church, we need to place their lives and doctrines within the context of each one's place in ecclesiastical history. To know when each lived and in what social context is imperative for sifting the essential principles of their spiritual legacy from the circumstances that surrounded their personal lives. This is important not only for religious, but for the guidance of the secular clergy and the laity.

Saint Augustine of Hippo (354 - 430)

We place our attention first on the time after the Church had emerged from the period of persecution under the pagan emperors and the beginning of freedom after Constantine in 313. Now freed from its oppression but needing its own new forms, the Church was tied into the structures of the Empire. During the times of persecution the pope was unable to communicate very effectively with his bishops, who were for the most part chosen by the local churches. Doctrinal errors had arisen, sometimes promoted by the bishops themselves, and had been widely disseminated. This was especially true in northern Africa. Freedom helped spread the heresies even

1

farther abroad. The need was apparent: a foundation of solid theological reasoning that would unify the Church's teaching authority and her holiness in the one Spirit.

The man raised up by God to have the greatest influence on the way the Church proclaims divine truth, in his and subsequent times, was one whose father Patricius was a Roman magistrate, a pagan, and whose mother was a holy Christian maiden named Monica. This man would lift himself from the paganism of Rome with its moral decay and philosophical sophistry into which he had become immersed. He would eventually reach the eminent position of Christian theologian and live a life of heroic virtue.

This man was Augustine, born in Thagaste, North Africa (present day Algeria), in 354. He would taste of the debauchery of Rome and become absorbed by its philosophies, until his search for truth brought him to attend the sermons of Saint Ambrose in Milan. Having found Christ through the Scriptures, especially in the letters of Saint Paul, he was baptized into the Christian faith in 387. Ordained to the priesthood in 390, he was raised to the episcopal dignity in 395 to assist the bishop of Hippo whom he succeeded soon after. For the next thirty-five years he gave himself to extensive writing and preaching in defense of the Catholic Faith against the prominent heresies of his day. These included Manicheism, Arianism, Donatism, and Pelagianism. He died in the year 430.

The depth of moral and intellectual confusion from which Augustine rose to his complete conversion in Christ is meticulously described and analyzed in his *Confessions*. He takes us on his journey of faith until he was totally absorbed into God through Christ. He does so with such depth of feeling that his subsequent place in the Church guarantees him a constant comparison with Saint Paul of Tarsus. As did Paul in the apostolic age, Augustine gave a stability to theological thought for the new age of evangelization. Fending off those who would destroy its unity in doctrine and charity, Augustine renewed and strengthened the Church of Christ for the golden age ahead, an era of holiness and scholarship that would last for centuries.

Augustine's moral and intellectual conversions ran parallel. As he understood the need for grace to overcome moral weakness, he learned that the source of truth is God. He reached that truth by allowing himself to be lifted up into the bond of love which is three Persons, until he could pray: "Our heart is restless, O God, until it rests in You."

His conversion began in earnest when in 386 he took up the New Testament and read the words of Paul in Romans 13:13-14: *Let us conduct ourselves properly as in the day, not in orgies and drunkenness, not in promiscuity and licentiousness, not in rivalry and jealousy. But put on the Lord Jesus Christ, and make no provision for the desires of the flesh.* He understood that the word of God must come first, and then only could his intelligence and reason come into play. The heart must first be converted before the mind can know God and comprehend the truth.

The power of the spiritual way of Saint Augustine shines forth in his *Rule.* His directives are very practical and pragmatic and very aware of the attraction to sin, even among men and women consecrated to the service of Christ and His Church. Yet the contrast to his other writings is startling. When he writes of love, Augustine lifts us up to lofty heights by the sublime nature of his thoughts, the need to see ourselves as a reflection of God's life in the distinct Persons of the Trinity. We are called to this relationship by baptism. He speaks often about Jesus as the source of Wisdom and the way to the Father. Yet the directions, admonitions and exhortations in his *Rule* focus on the weakness of the flesh, the constant temptation to a personal sense of superiority toward those whose lives we share in the community, and the subtleties of a piety which turns on itself. We have no theorist here.

Augustine's life struggle gave him this realistic attitude. In his search for truth he had been drawn to the Manicheans and the Neo-Platonists, but was weighed down by an insatiable desire for sensual pleasure (sexual and otherwise) and the delight of intellectual fantasy. After his conversion, he developed a profound respect for the dignity of the human person, body and soul, because the Word of God had assumed our human nature. Yet Augustine knew well that the forces of evil were never dormant. The purification of the senses was a constant need as well as firm discipline of the affections and the mind's curiosity. Hence his *Rule* stresses a restriction on freedom which is best exercised within the confines of community life. We cannot reflect, he believed, the life of the Triune God apart by ourselves. Truth is found by sharing this life with others.

As a guide in the spiritual life, Augustine keeps us focused on Jesus, the Word, through Whom we are drawn into the life of the Trinity, until we are "one mind and one heart in God." This requires discipline of our intellectual and physical powers, so we are not drawn away by the vagaries of our pride and sensuality from Him who is all Beauty and Wisdom. For Augustine, the cross of Jesus, a sign of His humility and obedience, was the key that opened the mind and soul to Truth.

Augustine's writings on the spiritual life were directed to various groups: those whom he had gathered around him to live together after the example of Jesus and the Apostles; women who were living in community in the pursuit of holiness and the service of charity; and hermits who had begun to form a life in community. From Augustine we have the foundation of a great gift to the Church. He gave us the fundamental principles of spiritual formation necessary to live in common with others who have consecrated their lives in service to the Church by vows of poverty, chastity and obedience, that is now uniformly called the religious life.

Saint Benedict of Nursia (480 - 543)

The idea of monasticism as a means of seeking God was steadily taking hold at the time of Augustine. The practice of reducing one's life to the necessities and dedicating oneself to prayer, study, and manual labor, while living apart from society, had begun in the deserts of Egypt with Anthony (c. 300), who was first a hermit and then a cenobite. Saint Basil the Great (329-379) provided the monastic movement in the East with the *Rule* that still serves today as a powerful influence in the Eastern Churches.

The movement revealed an intense desire of many for holiness. Its adherents were those not drawn to the apostolic life as was Augustine, but a life apart from the general populace. The idea soon spread from the East to the West. Unfortunately, a unifying force or principle was lacking, and before long there arose all kinds of strange forms and practices. Western monasticism was to receive its direction through the teachings of Saint Benedict, born in Nursia, Italy, in 480.

His family sent him to study in Rome in preparation for a secular career. The confusion and chaos of the political realities of the time, which affected the moral life of so many Christians, led Benedict to flee life in the city and become a hermit. He went off to a wilderness area called Subiaco. For three years he lived alone. Others, however, soon heard about his miracles and learned of his holy life. They began to seek his counsel. A community of monks nearby asked him to become their abbot, which they soon regretted because he expected them to make fundamental changes in their lifestyle. There was an attempt to poison him, and he left them and returned to his solitude. In time his reputation for holiness drew other men to ask if they might join him. He accepted some as companions. His expectations for the monks were not always appreciated and some difficulties arose. But the *Rule* which he wrote for the several monasteries he founded proved the correct formula. Benedict died in 543 at his monastery of Monte Cassino. His *Rule* reached to all parts of the western monastic world with the encouragement of Gregory the Great, who was pope from 590 to 604, and later through the efforts of the Emperor Charlemagne.

Benedict's *Rule* prescribed in detail the purpose of monastic life and how it should function, touching strongly on the structure of authority and the responsibilities of the monks to each other. The life of a monk was ordered, and was founded on an obedience to the abbot as one who took the place of Jesus. His life of prayer and work was directed toward the ultimate goal, union with God in the Kingdom of Heaven.

Thus through observance of the *Rule* the monks were an example to the Church of how the Son of God lived among us in obedience to His Father, offering Him constant adoration and praise. They were a prophetic presence in the local church, a constant reminder of man's responsibility to worship God and love his neighbor. The monks' concern for the people who lived in the vicinity of the monastery and their example of holiness served as an antidote to the often unchristian lives of secular princes and some clergy.

Into the Middle Ages

From the fifth to the twelfth centuries the influence of Augustinian and Benedictine spirituality was paramount, through the lives of Canons Regular in the apostolic order and monks in the contemplative order. Indeed there was need for the constant vigilance of the Church to preserve these institutions from human weakness and from secular interference. The renewal efforts of the monks of Cluny in the tenth century, the influence of Pope Gregory VII in the eleventh century, and the reforms in the twelfth century of Saint Bernard of Clairvaux (Cistercians), and Norbert of Xanten

(Premonstratensians) had the most wide reaching effect to this end. The spiritualities prevailed in varying forms and degrees. They fit perfectly the needs of the Church in calling to holiness persons in every station in life.

Times, however, were changing. By the twelfth century, schism had split Constantinople from Rome, the Crusades had drained the strength of Christendom, and the structures of the feudal system were beginning to weaken and disintegrate. The Holy Roman Empire, all Europe united by the one Faith and in loyalty to the Vicar of Christ, had become more a myth than a reality. The pope and bishops, because they possessed lands and armies, were too often seen more as worldly princes than spiritual leaders. The changing social conditions, and a growing merchant class often more wealthy than the nobility, pitted those with political power against those who had the power of money. There was much disillusionment with the hierarchy and clergy among both the privileged and the peasantry (*majores et minores*). The established structures of the Church were found wanting. Reform movements that often turned anti-clerical and heretical arose in many places. Scholars were critical; the poor were confused. Churchmen preached in vain because their lifestyles belied their teaching about a poor and crucified Savior.

Three figures emerged at the beginning of the 13th century to bring the Church to new life. The great Pope Innocent III sat on the chair of Peter (1198-1216). He convoked the Fourth Lateran Council (1215) to put his plans for reform into motion. Dominic and his followers were battling the heretics by solid scriptural preaching. Their simple and austere lives showed forth the sincerity of their beliefs, and defused the legitimate criticism of the Church's enemies. Francis and his followers showed Christ to the poor by living among them in lives of humble service. They preached not with eloquent theology but with simple sermons on vices and virtues.

The style of both served as an antidote to the conditions

of the times, and was a significant change from the ways of Augustine and Benedict. The Dominican and Franciscan friars were not limited to particular places as were canons, monks and nuns. They took religious life on the road, so to speak. Dogmatic and moral truths were proclaimed wherever the needs of the Gospel led them. Because they would live off their labors and by begging, they were called mendicants.

Saint Dominic Guzman (1170 - 1221)

Of noble Spanish birth, Dominic was prepared from his earliest years for a career in the Church, as priest and Canon Regular. By 1196, at the Cathedral of Osma, he was both. For seven years he fulfilled his responsibilities at home. By 1203 he began a series of journeys into France as a companion to his bishop and witnessed first hand the damage being done by the Albigensian heretics. Their teachings were rending the unity of Christ's Church. With the encouragement of the local bishop, he formed a group of preachers to protect the Church from the dangerous directions which these heretics were advocating in their efforts to purify her. They were demanding holiness of life in the priest as a prerequisite for the validity of the Masses he offered and the sacraments he conferred. A sinful bishop, it was said, need not be obeyed, much less the pope if his life was not Christ-like.

The band of preachers that Dominic assembled found success, not only because of their learned discourses but because their simple, prayerful and poor lives matched those of their adversaries. Dominic and his companions soon formed themselves into a community, supported by mortification and prayer according to the *Rule of Saint Augustine*. Necessary adaptations were made to respond to the exigencies of frequent travel. In due time, 1217, they were formally approved for the work of the Church as the Order of Preachers, just four years before Dominic's death.

Their motto was Truth (*Veritas*), and their lives would reflect Incarnate Wisdom. Through study of Scripture with the support of prayer in community, they would imitate the preaching of Christ and the Apostles who had wandered the countryside of Judea and Galilee. They would be mendicants, living off their labors and not from endowments, and would carry the message of Jesus into the towns and villages where His truth was not being heard.

Dominic's concern was to be faithful to the Truth that the Church had received from Christ. As the Apostles themselves had done, he too would go forth to preach, accompanied by those of like mind and calling. Dominic insisted that his followers focus on the Church's life, be obedient to her bishops, and thus be worthy preachers of the Gospel. As the Church they must expect to suffer, as Christ suffered and was often rejected. United in heart and spirit according to the mind of Christ, they strove to be faithful to the Truth which He had come to proclaim.

The Dominican Order of Friars, in its present Constitutions, expresses the purpose of its being: *The principal reason that we are gathered together is that we might dwell together in harmony and have one mind and one heart in God, that is to say, that we might be found perfect in charity.... Our Order is known to have been founded from the beginning expressly for preaching and the salvation of souls.... This end we ought to pursue, preaching and teaching from the abundance and fullness of contemplation in imitation of our most holy Father Dominic, who spoke only with God or of God for the benefit of souls.*

Saint Francis of Assisi (1182 - 1226)

At the same time that Dominic and his first companions (1206) had begun their campaign against the Albigensians in France, a young man by the name of Francis Bernardone had come to realize a call from Christ to leave the comfort and worldly success offered by his father's wealth as a cloth merchant of Assisi in Italy. He had lavished money on his friends in the pursuit of good times, earning himself the title: "King of youth." With a thirst for adventure, he determined to seek glory as a knight. His first try was during the war between Assisi and neighboring Perugia (1202), but he was captured and spent a year in prison. He survived because of his optimistic disposition, but the year was full of sickness and monotony. Ransomed by his father, he returned home with a new attitude.

Francis no longer had any interest in the frivolities of his youth. He began to appreciate what he had taken for granted: the wonder of God's creation. He aborted a second attempt for glory in battle, when he set out for Apulia with the campaign of Walter of Brienne, a famous warrior in the service of Pope Innocent III. In a vision he was made to realize that it is better to serve the "Master" and not his servant. A poor knight became the recipient of his grand military accouterments, and he returned to Assisi.

On a pilgrimage to Rome in order to reflect on his purpose in life, Francis was inspired to change clothes with a beggar on the steps of Saint Peter's Basilica. Being "one of the poor" even for a day thrilled him and gave him new insight into a reality which he had ignored: the many people who were not blessed with material advantages as he had been. Periods of prayer and time alone for reflection brought his relationship to God into focus, and he began to understand what was expected of him. His moment of conversion came one day as he was riding back to Assisi. He passed a leper on the road. On impulse, although totally nauseated, he galloped back, dismounted, and threw his arms around the man and kissed him on the cheek. He had recognized him as a brother of Jesus, an image of the poor and humble Son of God. Never again would another human being, no matter how "lowly" by reason of social position or physical condition, be treated with indifference or contempt.

Francis' way was made clear to him in 1206 while kneeling in prayer before a crucifix in the badly damaged wayside chapel of San Damiano, just outside Assisi. He heard the voice of Christ from the crucifix: "Go, repair my house which is falling down." He responded with enthusiasm and thereafter spent his time and money in fixing up the chapel, until his exasperated father, Pietro, dragged him before the local bishop, Guido. The father demanded that the bishop order his son to give up his foolishness and return to the decent life he once knew. The father also wanted him to pay for the bolts of cloth he had taken to trade for building materials.

When the bishop ordered the young man to do what his father asked, Francis removed his clothes, laid them at his father's feet, and declared to all the world that from henceforth he would call only God his father. He broke with his past and became one of the poor.

For two years Francis then lived as a hermit and continued to fix wayside chapels which needed repair, begging for his food and the materials he needed. He had also begun to speak in public places, exhorting all to a life of virtue and charitable concern for each other. He himself was caring for the lepers that lived in colonies outside the towns. In 1208, on February 24th, he heard the Gospel read on the feast of Saint Matthias: *Do not take gold or silver or copper for your belts; no sack for the journey, or a second tunic, or sandals, or walking stick* (Mt 10:9-10). These words of Christ to the Apostles before sending them out to preach became the guiding principle that Francis would live by. His simple prayer of praise would thereafter be: My God and my all!

The people of Assisi, meanwhile, considered Francis to be demented. But not all. Attracted by his kindness, sincerity and holy demeanor, other men, some nobles, including one priest, asked to join him in his way of life. Soon they numbered twelve. Since they were often taken for heretics (many of whom had adopted similar lifestyles), Francis traveled to Rome to ask the approbation of Pope Innocent III for their way of life. Henceforth, they became known as the Order of Lesser Brothers (*Friars Minor*).

Before long the friars numbered in the thousands, and Francis began sending them to other countries. By 1220 he had his first martyrs. Five friars had been sent to Morocco, but their open preaching infuriated the followers of Mohammed. They were soon killed. When their bodies were being brought home to Italy, they passed through Portugal where a young Canon Regular of Saint Augustine, on seeing what had happened to them, was inspired to become a Friar Minor. He is known to us today as Saint Anthony of Padua.

The friars' example had its greatest effect not on those who had reasoned themselves away from their Catholic Faith, but on those who lacked examples of the Christian life to whom they could relate. The majority of people were poor and uneducated. They could not be convinced to be faithful to Christ and His Church by the theological and scriptural arguments of scholars. But the simple life of the friars, echoing joy and peace, became the Gospel which they were unable to read. Many of them had become alienated from their Church leaders, who were often of the noble class and frequently involved in the struggle for power and property.

The life of Francis and his friars, which reflected the poverty and humility of Jesus, was a great contrast to the manner of life exhibited by many of the clergy. Yet the loyalty of Francis and the friars to Jesus, Son of God, showed itself in the profound reverence and obedience which they extended to priests, bishops, and the pope, who were Christ's own.

Francis died in 1226, two years after he had received in his hands, feet, and side the wounds of Christ crucified, a divine stamp of approval on the example he had set in living the life of Jesus, as revealed in the Gospel. Before long the Church was on her way back to unity: the Dominicans leading the way to doctrinal purity, the Truth that is Jesus; and the Franciscans showing what the Gospel truly means by living as Jesus did, as one of His people.

Into the Modern Era

By the sixteenth century western society had moved away from being an amalgamation of small kingdoms and principalities, joined into various alliances for survival or from family loyalties. Peoples of common heritage and language were being drawn together into nations with powerful monarchs. The cooperation of the state in matters ecclesiastical was becoming interference rather than a support.

The Church's moral influence was greatly weakened when Avignon in France became the seat of the papacy (1309-1377). This set the stage for open rebellion to her authority, and opposition to the person of the pope, who was thought to favor the French king and nobility. Competition arose between the pope and civic rulers in both Church and secular affairs.

When the popes again began to reside in Rome, unity in Christendom was by no means restored. A greater problem arose. Two and on occasion three cardinals laid claim to the Chair of Peter at the same time. This Great Schism lasted from 1378 to 1417. The moral confusion gave rise to questions about the very nature of the Church and efficacy of the sacraments. And there was a further distraction. Between 1447 and 1521 the so-called Renaissance Popes seemed more interested in returning Rome to her former glory than in rallying the Church to Gospel purity. They preferred to cultivate the arts and collect the treasures of ancient civilizations. The work of evangelization became almost exclusively dependent on the zeal and efforts of the local churches.

All this time the pope, as head of the papal states, was viewed too often as a secular ruler. His political actions in defense of his territory tarnished the image of the Vicar of Christ and the successor of Saint Peter. The situation was made worse by the scandalous personal lives of a few popes, some bishops, and numerous priests. Despite the efforts of notable Christian humanists of the age, such as Erasmus of Rotterdam, who was calling for reform from within, the most influential protagonists would separate themselves from the Church. They would take with them large segments of the people, even whole nations.

The apostasy began substantially in Germany with Martin Luther, a priest (1517), and with Ulrich Zwingli, also a priest, in Switzerland (1522). A Frenchman, John Calvin, beginning in Switzerland in 1536, organized Protestantism as a separate Church institution. His influence extended to Holland, England, Scotland, and America. He had some success in France. England severed allegiance to Rome when King Henry VIII was declared head of the Church in England by Parliament. Anglicanism was born in 1534 as a distinct 'catholic' Church.

Although moral issues were often on the surface, the very foundation of the Catholic Faith eventually came under attack: the supremacy of the Pope as the Vicar of Christ; the sacraments as instruments of grace; the Mass as a true sacrifice; the Eucharist as the true Body and Blood of Christ; and devotion to Mary as the Mother of God. Then too political expediency and the need for control over land and its resources more often than not became the motivating force for secular rulers to support the revolt from Rome. Even so, none could deny the need for a thorough reformation of the Church's life.

The renewal began slowly with the efforts of Hadrian VI in 1521. But the atmosphere in Rome was not conducive to any substantial change. The influence of the renaissance spirit, which was having such a debilitating effect on true reform, ended abruptly during the reign of Clement VII in 1527 with the sack of Rome by Emperor Charles V. Many viewed this action as the judgment of God.

A true renewal was effectively begun by Pope Paul III (1534-1549) with the reform of the Papal Court, especially by revitalizing the College of Cardinals with vigorous and saintly members. His efforts culminated in the convocation of the Council of Trent in 1545. The Church became mobilized for change, and the Catholic Reform Movement had begun in earnest.

Support for Church renewal on the political front came from the strongest and most faithful of the Catholic nations, Spain, which at this time had reached its zenith as a world power. From this people would come one whose movement would have the greatest influence in stabilizing and spreading the Catholic Faith throughout Europe and into the new lands being discovered.

Saint Ignatius of Loyola (1491 - 1556)

In the same year that Pope Paul III ascended the throne of Peter, a Spanish nobleman and six companions at the University of Paris vowed their lives to God in service to His Church. Their spiritual bond would become in time the nucleus of the Society of Jesus.

Ignatius was brought up for a career as a courtier. At the age of thirty that lifestyle came to a sudden end when he received a leg wound at Pamplona in a battle with the French. During his convalescence, the lack of any reading material to his liking forced him to fill his time with all that was at hand — the *Life of Christ* by Ludolf of Saxony and a book on the lives of various saints. He was especially taken up with Saint Dominic, his countryman, and Saint Francis of Assisi. A new challenge surged in his soul, one that led him into spiritual combat. His first resolve was to make a pilgrimage to Jerusalem.

But first he went to the famous abbey at Montserrat, where he surrendered his horse, armor and sword at the feet of Our Lady. Then, on his way to board a ship at Barcelona, he planned a stop at the town of Manresa for some days of prayer in preparation for the journey. Instead his stay lasted almost a year. During this time, as his soul struggled with spiritual purgation and awareness, he found strength from reading the Scriptures and the *Imitation of Christ*. He recognized that he was in a battle against evil and in preparation for the defense of the Kingdom of God. The account which he kept of his daily readings and meditations has become the renowned *Spiritual Exercises*, which have continued to be an integral part of the first phase of training for his followers until the present day. Countless others, cleric and lay, have also found them an indispensable first step as they set out on a path of serious conversion to the service of Christ.

Ignatius remained in Jerusalem only a short time (1523). He returned to Spain with the determination to become a priest. For five years he studied in Barcelona and Alcalá, and eventually set out for the University of Paris to study theology. While there he had great influence on several fellow-students, and they were persuaded to undertake his *Exercises*. One was a priest, Peter Faber, and another the future Saint Francis Xavier.

By 1534 a group of seven had formed a close spiritual friendship. On August 15th that year, during Mass, they vowed to go to Jerusalem, and from there work for the salvation of the infidels. If this were not possible, they would go to Rome and offer their services to the pope. Rome it turned out to be. The year 1537 found them heading toward the Eternal City. In Venice, the remaining six were ordained priests.

Ignatius appealed to Pope Paul III that he commission them for the work of the Church. In 1540, calling themselves the "Company of Jesus," they were formally recognized as an Order with a twofold purpose, namely, to come to the defense of the Church wherever it was being assailed, and to propagate the Faith at home and abroad. Francis Xavier had already left for India, and later on he led a group of Jesuits (now called) to Japan. The Americas too would soon be invaded by this new army of Christ. By the death of Ignatius in 1556, their number had reached 1000, and their missionary and educational efforts were becoming legendary.

Besides the Jesuits, many new orders surfaced in the

Church during the sixteenth and seventeenth centuries, as well as movements of reform among the established religious communities. Each had its special impact on the spiritual life of the faithful. However, Saint Ignatius and the Society of Jesus made the greatest contribution to a sense of stability and purpose in the Church's mission of evangelization. They led the charge in the counter-reformation, and their every effort was inspired by the battle-cry: *For the Greater Glory of God.*

In addition, previously existing orders were returning to their contemplative traditions and to greater austerity of life. Chief among these was the venerable Order of Carmel, formed by Saint Albert, bishop of Jerusalem, in the eleventh century from the many hermits who lived on Mount Carmel in Palestine, a mountain associated with the prophet Elijah and his confrontation with the prophets of Baal. The one who returned the Carmelite Order to the practice of the pristine rule, and whose influence was felt beyond her own reform movement, also came from Spain, the mystic Teresa.

Saint Teresa of Avila (1515 - 1582)

She was born into a prominent family at the same time Martin Luther was about to cause a major split in Christendom. From her earliest years Teresa felt challenged by accounts of the saints and martyrs. She even attempted at the age of seven to head for Africa with her brother to die for the Faith.

After her mother's death when Teresa was thirteen years of age, her pious childhood turned into a distracted adolescence. She was a vivacious young woman — alert, sensitive, and taken to vanities and romantic dreaming. A very concerned father sent her to study with the Augustinian nuns, with whom she stayed for almost two years.

The young lady returned home because she had gotten seriously ill. But the experience away caused her to rediscover her interest in prayer and the imitation of the saints. At the age of twenty and against her father's wishes, she began her life as a religious in the Carmelite Convent of the Incarnation in Avila. Shortly after her profession of vows, however, she became sick again and returned to her father's house to receive care. Treatments were virtually useless, and she almost died. The experience deepened her attraction to prayer and her desire to know the love of Jesus.

In 1540 Teresa returned to Incarnation convent with a paralysis that remained for almost three years. She suddenly received a miraculous cure. This miracle, which she credited to Saint Joseph, brought her to the attention of many outside the convent and she was drawn into their worldly concerns. Her prayer life was neglected as she conformed herself to the frivolous social life of her friends. This period of mediocrity continued for more than fifteen years. At the age of thirty-nine, grace began to work as she realized how far she had drifted from her initial fervent spirit. She would again seek to correspond to God's love through prayer and penance.

Teresa restructured her life to one of greater austerity, gave herself over to meditative prayer, and sought spiritual direction. This latter was often not very helpful, and her attempts to follow sometimes contradictory advice proved disturbing. Her new ways began to irritate many of the other nuns, and ridicule was often her lot. For a time she received no consolation in prayer, although on other occasions she received mystical graces. Her meditations on the sufferings of Christ on the cross gave her the will to persevere. She felt a special kinship with the penitents Augustine and Mary Magdalene.

Teresa received help from followers of several spirituality traditions. Some of her more helpful advisors were from the newly formed Jesuit Order. A Dominican confessor assured her that the visions she had received from the Lord were authentic. A Franciscan, Saint Peter of Alcantara, encouraged her in her resolve to return to the original *Rule* of Carmel that was in place before 1432. He helped her obtain the approval of the bishop. With the reluctant permission of her superiors, she and four other nuns established a new foundation in Avila, the convent of Saint Joseph. In a short time other nuns felt called to the strict way and joined her.

Saint Joseph's began in 1562 and continued for five years under Teresa's direction. The nuns observed poverty with strict enclosure. In 1567 the General of the Carmelite Order of men, under whose authority the nuns lived, was impressed by what he saw. He made it his concern to encourage Teresa to develop other foundations. She was also asked to help in the renewal of the life of the Carmelite friars.

During the next twenty years, with frequent virulent opposition from civil and ecclesiastical sources, she founded fifteen convents of the reform. With the support of Saint John of the Cross, a Carmelite friar, she helped establish communities of friars who wanted to live their former austerity and be devoted to prayer. The reform had so taken hold and spread that in 1593 the Holy See recognized two separate branches of the Carmelite Order. Teresa's reform (men and women) became the Order of Discalced (barefoot) Carmelites.

As one might expect, Teresa spent much time instructing her nuns with letters and other writings that covered every aspect of the spiritual life, with special emphasis on prayer. She recounted her own spiritual experiences in her *Autobiography* and described the journey toward union with God in her *Interior Castle*. Saint John of the Cross, her companion in reform and suffering, also wrote extensively on mystical theology. They both have been declared Doctors of the Church.

Teresa died in 1582, when the effects of the Council of Trent and the Catholic Reform Movement were taking hold. The Church everywhere had benefited from her influence in strengthening the religious spirit of her age. In the following centuries the emergence of many new religious orders and congregations of men and women would bring untold blessings to the Church. These new communities would pursue works of Christian charity in education and in concern for the poor, the sick, and other sufferers. Their efforts would not be limited by the rules of enclosure nor the confines of their home countries.

* * * *

The life of the Church has been energized since the beginning by the work and spirit of countless holy men and women. All have been raised up to bring needed stimulus to the People of God. The majority made their mark in localized and specific situations. The lives and works of not a few, however, were felt in every place, and are having an effect up to the present day. The six whose lives are outlined above, within the appropriate historical context, have been the most broadly influential. They must never be considered just relics of past glory.

In the frustrations we might feel in the struggle to bring the Church to renewal in this age, we ought not to pine for the arrival of a new spiritual giant. The treasures which we already have must be rediscovered, and be made to invigorate every area of ecclesial life. The Church is always holy, and holiness is the fountainhead of true Church renewal in any age.

CHAPTER TWO

TO COMPARE IS TO COMPREHEND

The Augustinians and Benedictines, the Dominicans and Franciscans, the Jesuits and Carmelites all flourish today. Their very longevity compels us to give them attention. The spiritualities which they embody have had an enormous impact on the holiness of the Church. They have guided the spiritual lives of countless souls who were not members of these Orders, nor had ever taken vows in religious life. These distinct traditions of spirituality are having great influence to this day, long after the saints whose lives and teachings inspired them have died. Indeed, the civil, social and ecclesiastical conditions that brought them to prominence no longer exist.

That is the challenge. The spiritualities we have from them are in evidence everywhere. Changing circumstances have brought about new forms and variations since the sixteenth century. Particular needs have inspired holy men and women to found new congregations. Subsequent foundations have given a more focused emphasis to one or the other aspect of an inherited tradition, in response to a very particular apostolic need. None of the later founders, however, have had the broad influence of the *Great Six*.

In view of the Second Vatican Council's call for the renewal of religious life, it behooves us to sift their personal and unique experiences from the historical circumstances in which each saint lived and to bring them into the present age. We need to discover the essence of their spiritual teachings in order to delineate the reasons which make their spiritualities different from each other. This is our supposition, that their ways of holiness are each quite unique. Their present day disciples are called to play distinct roles in the renewal of the Church in our generation. How account otherwise for their separate survival through many tumultuous times in their respective histories? Other orders and reforms of more recent origins no longer exist. Those that still do and continue to bless the Church's life essentially reflect, I believe, the spirituality of one of our six saints in new forms.

We have briefly reviewed the historical circumstances and personal responses from each saint's life. The second step is to determine any similarities between some of them, or even all of them. We must also note the differences between those who may be similar in some ways. By making comparisons and accentuating the differences we will be able to preserve the distinctions between the saints themselves and their followers today. There are different gifts but the same Spirit by which the holiness of the Church is advanced.

We are dealing with the renewal of the Church in two broad areas: purity of doctrine (the true Faith) and moral integrity (living the Gospel). Both, of course, are integral to a holy life, and they are not separated in any of our saints' lives. What we do note is that their lives focus on one or the other, on the doctrinal or the moral. On one side we have Augustine, Dominic, and Ignatius. On the other there are Benedict, Francis, and Teresa.

The form which their spiritual lives took had unique characteristics, which directly flowed from each one's purpose. Augustine was the churchman *par excellence*, leading his diocese and teaching his people. Dominic and Ignatius were called to evangelize in very many places, so their activity was more far-reaching. Francis, too, wandered far and wide, but his reason was to be an instrument of peace wherever he brought his Gospel lifestyle. Benedict and Teresa founded monasteries, where contemplation would reign and charity would be its fruit.

The personalities of our sainted brothers and sisters were also quite distinctive. The mischievous and ambitious Augustine passed through a dissolute youth and young manhood before he set out on a path that led to the priesthood and episcopacy. Dominic, solidly virtuous and serious minded, had the priesthood as his goal from his earliest years. Benedict, of a pious and trusting nature, began studies in Rome for a worldly career. His disillusionment with the evil he witnessed brought about a change of mind and he left Rome to seek the contemplative life in solitude. Teresa, a pious dreamer, sensitive and stubborn, was looking for holiness from her childhood. It was a personal goal. However, having succumbed to her vanity, she passed eighteen years of her religious life in mediocrity. Yet both Teresa and Benedict became instruments in the renewal of religious life. And then there was Francis, the fun-loving and frivolous son of a wealthy merchant. He attempted to become a knight, not because he had a disposition to fight but as a means of obtaining honor and public distinction. His recognition would come later as a leader of poor men. Ignatius, however, was bred to be a soldier. He was high-spirited and courageous, disciplined and proud. He turned from his pursuit of military honors to lead an army of scholars and missionaries for the glory of Christ and the spread of His Kingdom. Yet both Francis and Ignatius had a spirit of adventure that, once turned around, brought into the Church two entirely new forms of religious life.

Their diverse temperaments fitted the work God had called them to do. Can we picture Augustine living the poverty of Francis, wandering about preaching simple sermons and begging his food? Benedict the Abbot, concerned with stability in the life of his monks, was not up to organizing a crusade for the Faith as Dominic did. Teresa, the woman, probably as strong-willed as any of the others, could not have brought about a reform from within if she had to focus on a world-wide mission of spiritual conquest, as Ignatius the soldier envisioned. Yet they each had what was needed to fulfill the special hope that grew from their respective experiences, and bring to the Church differing brands of holiness.

The journey of any Christian toward great holiness begins with a conversion. Augustine had to turn from a life of sin. Benedict could not find God in the corruption of Roman life where he had gone to study, so he fled to live in solitude and austerity. Dominic needed to uproot himself from the secure life of a Canon Regular to venture to places where the Faith was under siege and to adapt himself to uncertain traveling and living conditions. Francis gave up a carefree life and material comfort to live in a manner reminiscent of the poor and humble Son of God. Ignatius went from the discipline needed to be a good soldier in defense of a material kingdom to the more vigorous training required to be a soldier of the spirit. Teresa gave up the comfort of a mediocre religious life to challenge others by word and example in a total surrender of herself to Jesus, the crucified Savior. Benedict, Dominic, and Teresa took a simple right angle turn in their journey toward the fulfillment of God's will. Augustine, Francis, and Ignatius turned completely around to go in the opposite direction. They did not become, however, entirely new people. They brought with them everything they were before, i.e., their own cultural, emotional and temperamental makeup. But now all was focused on a specific end, the following of Jesus on the path to which He had beckoned them.

As our saints converged on the New Jerusalem, they might be said to have come by different routes or means: by sea (Augustine) or land (Teresa); over mountains (Benedict) or across the plains (Dominic); by foot (Francis) or by wagon (Ignatius). Each way had its dangers; each one needed the spirit of fortitude; each traveler needed similar strengths. For all of them the cross of Jesus was the guiding star. The virtues of humility and obedience, of charity and constancy in the face of opposition was evident in all. Each one, indeed, was a Catholic saint.

All needed the grace of the same Holy Spirit. As flowers of different species, they grew in the same garden — the Church. The same sacraments nourished them; they grew in the same soil and were united in loyalty and obedience to the authority of the Vicar of Christ, the Pope. They breathed with the same spirit of prayer, drawn upwards beyond themselves by the Sun of Justice and Truth, the Son of God made Man. They all recognized that they had been redeemed from sin through His death. Their common goal was union with Jesus.

In other ways besides matters spiritual, the six were very much alike. All enjoyed the advantages of education, since they came from the privileged ranks of society. All six could have pursued very successful worldly careers. Precisely because of their social rank, however, God was able to call them to the special work He wanted of them, to produce an effect that would be broad and long-lasting. Their education and social contacts were most valuable to further the very works they could accomplish only after they first abandoned their former ways of life.

We can find similarities and differences also in the place the *Great Six* had within the Church herself. Augustine, Dominic, and Ignatius were priests, with varying expertise as theologians. They were, therefore, much concerned with the propagation of the Faith, with writing, teaching, and doctrinal preaching. Their program of life might be thought of as eminently pragmatic, to make them better equipped spiritually and intellectually to be involved in the active ministry of souls. Their spiritualities inseparably linked personal holiness with the apostolic life. Benedict, Francis, and Teresa on the other hand were far from illiterate, but they were not university graduates. Their concern was not ostensibly to teach by words (although they did leave us writings), but to demonstrate a lifestyle that could bring one into close union with Jesus. Any consequent acts of charity or evangelizing efforts resulted from this nearness to Jesus and became an integral part of their spiritual doctrine.

This distinction between a *pragmatic* spirituality and one that is primarily *charismatic* is not just a subtlety. The stress is placed on either activity or contemplation — with neither, however, standing alone. Their vital connection is readily understood and the emphasis appears logical when we recall the three periods of history which our saints were called to influence. In the 4th-5th centuries the need for doctrinal purification called forth Augustine. Benedict arrived soon after to bring about reformation of the monastic life. Dominic in the 13th century set himself against the heresies which were dividing the Church, and Francis in the same period renewed the Church's moral vitality by the example of Christ's poverty and humility with his new form of Gospel-style religious life. In another era, the 16th century, Ignatius led the Company of Jesus in strengthening the Faith among those who professed it, and carrying the Christian message to new places. At the same time Teresa brought us the renewed message that prayer makes the work of evangelization effective and that contemplation is the goal of the Christian life. Their respective methods of spiritual formation and direction reflected the work they had been raised up to accomplish in the Church.

Never Alone on the Way to Holiness

Since all our saints were "founders" of ecclesiastical movements, they instinctively followed the example of the early Christians and developed forms of a "common life" among their followers. They felt bonded, of course, as are all the baptized in the community of faith which is the Church. But they knew the need of a special unity with those of similar mind and purpose.

This need to "be of one mind and one heart" called for a sharing of temporal goods, time for common prayer, mutual support in physical needs, cooperation in apostolic and charitable responsibilities and a certain order in the details of daily life and work. The love of God and the desire to do His will would be the binding force in the relationship of the members of each Order to one another, but in practice it also needed a promise of obedience to a human representative who would direct their efforts.

All our saintly six placed great stress on community as a most important component in the pursuit of holiness, to facilitate the practice of virtue and to attain union with Jesus. Yet the form of common life each developed was markedly different from the others. In general, we might say that Augustine, Dominic, and Ignatius considered their followers as an apostolic band and developed their community life according to the model of Jesus and the Apostles in relationship to each other. But there were notable differences even here, as we shall see. The general model of community life as put forth by Benedict, Francis, and Teresa was that of a family relationship. Yet even among them there were profound differences. To analyze and compare the different kinds of community life that our saints envisioned for their followers is a good place to begin in order to understand their uniqueness.

Augustine embodied much of the monastic tradition in the exhortations found in his *Rule*, with great emphasis on prayer, study, and mutual concerns by the community's members for each others' physical and spiritual well-being. But the canons were not monks, and so there were notable exceptions. First of all, although he calls for a simple life, without ostentation, the ascetical practices of monks were lacking. Most importantly of all, however, was the role of the superior in the life of the community. In the monastery the abbot is completely in charge, and all owe him full obedience and the respect due to a father. For Augustine the relationship of his followers to each other was more like close *friends*. The superior was first among equals, having responsibilities rather than authority. We remember that Augustine formed his first community by gathering around him friends who shared his apostolic life and on whom he could count for support. He needed the trust of people with whom he was comfortable and with whom he had chosen to live, in order to seek their counsel and for them to protect him from his own follies.

The bond of the Augustinian community is one of deep friendship in the support of a common apostolic life, namely, to fulfill the mission of Jesus and His Church: to teach and sanctify. *I no longer call you slaves, because a slave does not know what his master is doing. I have called you friends, because I have told you everything I have heard from my Father* (Jn 15:15).

Benedict places the leadership of his community in the hands of an abbot: *An Abbot who is worthy to be over a monastery should always remember what he is called, and live up to the name of Superior. For he is believed to hold the place of Christ in the monastery, being called by a name of His, which is taken from the words of the Apostle: "You have received a Spirit of adoption as sons, by virtue of which we cry, 'Abba' — Father!"* (Rule, ch. 2). The *Rule* lays upon him heavy responsibilities with appropriate authority to fulfill them.

The monks lived under the direction of the abbot, who was their teacher. He was responsible for discipline and could punish a monk who was disobedient to him or to the *Rule*. Benedict reminds each monk in chapter seven: *that God is always looking at him from heaven, that his actions are everywhere visible to the divine eyes and are constantly being reported to God by the Angels*. Benedictines see themselves as *sons*, whose prayer and work give honor and glory to God, their heavenly Father.

Dominic formed his community to preach against heresy. His Order stressed preaching, teaching, and writing as essential elements of the apostolic life. He had in effect brought to the Church a new form of religious life, retaining nonetheless the *Rule of Saint Augustine* and drawing from his experience as a Canon Regular. In his new way of life liturgical prayer and study would remain a high priority. However, preachers travel. They do not have the stability that monastic life provides. Therefore, the internal structures and operation of the new Order needed greater flexibility. The pursuit of holiness became a prayerful preparation to go forth and preach with fidelity to Christian truth and with a lifestyle whose simplicity and spirit of mortification would have positive influence on souls and make them ready for conversion.

The mission of the new religious was not localized, as with Canons Regular and monks. This difference alone demanded a new concept of authority. Their material needs were not provided for by endowments, but as mendicants they depended on the generosity of the people. The individual Dominican exercised greater responsibility in the mutual support of their common enterprise. The Master General who governed the Order and coordinated its apostolic efforts was not present to each friar daily as the abbot was to his monks.

Because their call is to know Jesus better, as the one who leads us to the Father and who must be proclaimed to the world, Dominicans are united as *students* in a school of contemplation. Together they learn the divine mysteries. They become identified with Christ as priest, who is our way to the Father, who is the Truth to be preached, and whose death brought us life. *I am the way, the truth and the life; no one goes to the Father except through me* (Jn 14:6).

Francis also brought to the Church a new form of religious life, which like that of Dominic did not restrict its members to a particular place. Indeed, this "poor man of Assisi" exhorted his followers to live in the world as "pilgrims and strangers." He began his new life alone, associating with lepers and caring for them, working for or begging food and shelter. When he began to follow the Gospel injunction to *take nothing for your journey* and to reach out by simple preaching to encourage ordinary people to a renewed life in Christ, then others became interested in joining him. He called himself and his band the 'lesser brothers' (*friars minor*) because they must be identified with the simple people.

The brothers were to "serve each other in poverty and humility" and "to treat each other as members of one family" and "to cherish and love him who is his brother according to the spirit" (Rule VI). Those who guided the brothers were to be called ministers since Jesus came "to serve and not be served." No one was to preach unless approved by his minister, and then in simple words. Where the bishop might object to their presence, they were to go elsewhere. They honored and respected all priests, no matter how poor, ignorant, or even sinful. Their conduct toward the clergy became an antidote to the influence of the heretics who denied obedience to any bishop or priest whose conduct was deemed un-Christlike.

The Order of Francis of Assisi was a *brotherhood* of poor men, whose preaching was to be more by example than by learned discourse.

Ignatius was a man of action, disciplined in the pursuit of an ideal, and passionate in loyalty to his cause. From the moment of his call to the standard of Jesus at the age of 31 in 1522 until his ordination to the priesthood 15 years later, he never wavered in his response to God's will for him. He had to be ready — no matter how long it took. Victory went to the strong and prepared.

Those attracted to him were of like mind. With the six men who had in 1534 promised to give themselves to the service of Jesus and His Church, plus three others who joined them later, he went to Rome where they were commissioned as the Company of Jesus by the Vicar of Christ, Pope Paul III. Their mission had begun.

Ignatius and his community had a strong sense of fidelity to Church leadership as to Christ, and also to each other. They prepared with rigorous training to face great odds together and to undertake special assignments that called for a steadfast purpose. Success also demands great coordination of individual efforts. And as in any struggle, a sudden change of circumstances presents a challenge for an immediate response, which is no task for the faint-hearted.

Very broad and intense apostolic cooperation marks the style of the Society of Jesus and has resulted in many great works and institutions becoming influential parts of the Church's life throughout the world. However, the community life of Jesuits allows for, and often encourages, personal initiatives. In their common life the followers of Ignatius of Loyola project a profound loyalty to each other as *companions of Jesus* and friends in the Lord.

Teresa of Avila has given us a body of literature on the contemplative life that covers every possible nuance of the divine relationship to which we are called. She recognizes the sometimes subtle obstacles which our human condition, full of pride and spiritual ambition, places in our way — even when we claim to work for God and His glory. The intimacy of the cloistered Carmelite life provided ample opportunities for the practice of detachment from the world of our own will. The nuns lived as sisters in the same household under obedience to a Mother Prioress. Teresa's reform returned them to the framework of prayer, poverty, and fasting, which allowed the spirit of God to enter the soul and lift her up into Himself, which is contemplation.

The form of community life that Teresa espoused reveals fundamental points of similarity to monasticism, especially in the stress on liturgical prayer and obedience to the will of a superior as mother. Even the goal is the same — union with God. The relationship, however, of the nuns to each other is quite different. They live not so much as daughters of the heavenly Father, but as *daughters of Mary*, who is the spouse of the Holy Spirit and mother of the Son of God. Teresa's great personal devotion to Saint Joseph, Mary's husband, reflected a sense of kinship with the Holy Family. Her first reformed convent, named for Saint Joseph, had the family of Nazareth as its model, which best describes the personal relationships within the Carmelite Order since then.

* * * *

We have begun our comparisons by speaking first about the purpose of each saint's life in their call from God during a specific chaotic historical period, and then about the consequent form of community life which each purpose demanded. We have yet to say anything about the spiritualities that grew from these dual roots of purpose and community. Spirituality concerns itself with the practice of virtue and is a matter of grace building on nature. We need to look for a grace principle that motivated six distinct personalities to give their lives to Jesus. They were different kinds of people, and, drawn by grace and temperament, they viewed Him through distinct prisms of experience. The results were amazingly varied. To this wonder we want to be faithful.

We remember that we are speaking also of those who follow the separate ways of our six saints from a vocation in the secular state, and who live under disparate social and ecclesial circumstances. We need, therefore, to go to the essence of each one's spiritual example so that it is universally applicable. Therefore, we must ask: what is necessary, and absolutely indispensable, in order to imitate the very distinct life of any of our saints in whatever place, and under whatever circumstances, and in whatever state of life that we find ourselves as we strive for holiness?

CHAPTER THREE

THE MANY FACES OF JESUS

We are speaking about different spiritualities, different forms of motivation toward a common goal, i.e., oneness with Jesus, our Lord and God. To be valid, they must encompass all aspects of the spiritual life, and cover every element of the Gospel. A particular motivation to fulfill a very specific action cannot be called a spirituality, even when it is performed under the influence of grace. Today we hear such well-meaning expressions as the spirituality of healing, but we also have the absurd, e.g., the spirituality of sports. The issue is confused when we speak about the spiritual life of a particular individual, such as, "the spirituality of Thomas Merton" or "the spirituality of Mother Teresa." I even have trouble with "Marian spirituality" because all authentic spiritualities must be Marian, just as all authentic spiritualities must be Christocentric and fundamentally Trinitarian.

To be precise, for example, the expression should be Augustinian spirituality, i.e., the spirituality inspired by and given to us by Saint Augustine, rather than the spirituality of Saint Augustine. We do not want to be constrained by time and place.

The Varied Aspects of Relationships

As intelligent beings we always have reason for our action or inaction. The reason may be totally selfish, or be a response to love. Usually in our imperfect state it is somewhere in-between. From the moral perspective, if the action is fundamentally selfish, we call it sin. If it is prompted by love, we call it virtue. If our lives are built on the love of God, we speak of supernatural virtue.

The motivation which helps us to overcome our fallen nature's propensity toward evil may be as ungallant as the fear of hell. The measure of a response to goodness may come from a sense of obligation toward our Creator, but when it is guided by a generous love of Jesus, we call it holiness. When our generosity is total, we call it sanctity. The program or system we follow to maintain a steady progress in holiness toward the goal of sanctity is called a spirituality. And that is what we are speaking about here.

In the Church we have six very different spirituality traditions. All are intrinsically woven into the fabric of the Church's holiness and her devotional practices. Everyone who is sincere about living the Gospel in true disciple-union with Jesus chooses one or the other without always knowing which one is being followed, i.e., without being able to give it a name. Any nuance or emphasis which is added by an individual, including subsequent founders of religious orders or congregations, will reflect a difference of experience or a unique and sometimes limited purpose. A "new" spirituality may be known by a different name because it has a very specific priority, but it will be radically Augustinian or Benedictine, Dominican or Franciscan, Ignatian or Teresian.

Since all of us, as Christians, have received the life of God, and were baptized into the death and resurrection of Jesus, we are members of the one Church. We join in offering the same Eucharistic Sacrifice as the central act of our faith-filled lives, and receive the same Sacraments. We live in obedience to God's will in accord with the state of life to which He has called us. We serve Him in humility, share His cross, and are men and women of prayer. Whatever may be our spirituality, we are traveling in the same direction. The questions we face then are: Why do we do things differently? Are our differences notable and important to the Church? What is the reference point of these differences when so much of our Christian lives converge?

We must begin, of course, with Jesus, since our goal is to be one with Him and to join in the fulfillment of His mission. We have responded to His call: "Come, follow me!" and we follow Him with joy. But He will also send us off to work: "Go, teach all nations what I have commanded you!" We cannot simply spend our time sitting at His feet, as Mary the sister of Martha did when Jesus visited their home. Yet He did say that Mary had chosen the better part. The first command is to "come!" The second is to "go!" And there is a third: "Come away and rest awhile!" Jesus has set out on His journey. We follow Him as His disciples; He sends us off to do His work as His apostles; and then He calls us back to be with Him as His friends.

Jesus is our Way ("follow me"), our Truth ("go and teach"), and our Life ("come away and rest"). We must, therefore, make our first concern this personal relationship to Jesus. That relationship will determine our lifestyle. That is why we want to examine the special relationship of each of our saints to the Lord Jesus. Who was Jesus to Augustine? Was He someone different to Dominic and Ignatius? All three had responded with notable enthusiasm to the command "go and teach." Francis, on the other hand, was more interested in "following Jesus" by imitating His life. Benedict and Teresa were content with having "the better part."

We do not wish to imply that our saints, in emphasizing one command, were ignoring the others. All the commands are linked and Jesus intended that we obey them all. Yet the differing emphases by our saints indicate a different understanding of their relationship to Jesus. We need to speak about this more, but first we want to be clear about the meaning of relationship.

Relationships belong to the very nature of life, beginning with God, in whose image we have all been created. In God we have the eternal relationship between the Father and the Son with the Holy Spirit. Each is a distinct Person from the others, yet they form the One Being, the One Life. It is the reason that we are able to say: God is Love. So too we have been created for love and love flows from relationships. From the account in the Book of Genesis (2:18) we have God saying: "It is not good for the man to be alone. I will make a suitable partner for him." He creates for Adam a woman who would be his wife. They shall become one flesh and beget new life, and thus begins a new relationship. No longer will they be just man and woman, husband and wife. Now it is a three person relationship: father to mother and both to child. Three persons, one being, i.e., a family. And this relationship, too, is eternal, unchangeable.

There are many words which indicate in themselves the extent of the link between members in the human "family chain," beginning with father, mother, child. We notice that each word implies the others, indicating a relationship. Father implies mother and child; mother implies father and child; son or daughter implies father and mother. Think about uncle, aunt, cousin, brother, sister, grandmother, grandfather, niece, nephew, etc. Each one suggests an intrinsic bond with at least two other persons, sometimes many more. By our birth we are automatically connected forever to many people. Other relationships develop because of marriage decisions of which we had nothing to say either, such as, son-in-law and step-mother. There are also legal relationships, such as those which come into being when a child is adopted. Thus we see that some relationships are permanent, others quasi-permanent, and still others are temporal and of our own choice, such as friend, team-mate, or employee.

Our relationship to any individual will set the stage for any conversation, no matter what the subject may be. And we will respond to anything which that person might ask of us with due consideration to that relationship. A man holds a conversation much differently with his wife, his mother, his father, his children, his male friends, with women, etc. A mother speaks to her daughter as a mother to a daughter, even though she might recognize that her daughter has become a very successful career woman or be the mother of eight children. My own mother was very proud that her son was a priest, and she always called me Father when anyone else was present. Privately, just between us, I was still her boy growing up, and she chatted with me and advised me accordingly. No surprise. It is human nature. Whatever else a person may be in the eyes of others, the fundamental relationship with any individual is the source from which all expressions flow.

Human beings are not composites. We recognize many facets of the same personality. However, we do focus on the one aspect into which all the others blend. We center all our attention on the fundamental relationship we perceive ourselves to have with the individual.

Thus our Lord, Jesus Christ, can be considered from many points of view: the Second Person of the Blessed Trinity, Mary's son who became my brother, my Redeemer who died on the cross to save me from sin, my Master who formed His Church on Peter to bring all people to salvation, my Teacher who has sent me forth to proclaim the Good News, etc. Jesus is each of these, and He is all of them. None may be separated from any of the others, since we speak about the one Person, Jesus. But, as human beings, we are compelled to have a focal point that will result from our experiences and temperament. Hence, I propose that this is precisely how we can understand the difference between our six saints and their methods as they search to know God. Each placed the focus of their affection on a separate aspect of the Person who is Jesus. Let me show how I have come to understand each saint's uniqueness from the perspective of "focus."

Experience Begets Perspective

Augustine lived and worked in a time of great doctrinal confusion that affected ecclesial harmony to the detriment of souls. The question in dispute was most fundamental: Who was Jesus? Arius, a priest, answered that Jesus was not God, but a created son of God, effectively negating the Trinity. Nestorius, patriarch of Constantinople, claimed that Jesus was both a human as well as a divine person. The Monophysite heresy, championed by Abbot Eutyches of Constantinople, denied the humanity of Christ altogether, declaring that Jesus was not a human being at all, but a mere visible manifestation of the Second Person of the Blessed Trinity.

In combating these heresies, Augustine produced some of his greatest theological works. He was totally vindicated when the Council of Ephesus in 431 declared that Mary must be called the Mother of God, since Jesus was the Son of God, a divine Person. She was not the mother of a human person, nor just the mother of Christ in His human nature. The Council of Chalcedon in 451 left no doubt who Jesus is by stating unequivocally that He is truly the Son of God, the Second Person of the Blessed Trinity, who had assumed a human nature through Mary. He was one Person (divine) who possessed two distinct natures, one divine and the other totally human. He was true God and true Man.

Augustine also wrote many renowned works to counteract the influence of the monk, Pelagius who had denied the need of grace through baptism, declaring that the sin of Adam and Eve had affected only their own relationship to God, not that of their descendants. A person could be saved simply by willing it. Hence, there was no need for Christ to redeem us. His life and death should be seen only as an example to encourage us to be faithful. Augustine's own life, however, was proof enough to him for the need and power of grace. He had been helpless to change without it. He had found Christ in the writings of Saint Paul, who eloquently lays out the whole doctrine of redemption in so many places.

So we might consider it a supernatural consequence of his theological defense of the person and mission of Jesus that Augustine would focus his attention in prayer on the Son of God made Man. He had learned very well that Jesus was the way to the Father, and that through Jesus we receive the grace of the Holy Spirit. Therefore, we enter the life of the Blessed Trinity, of God, through the humanity of the Son, having become adopted children of God by reason of our baptism. Augustine identified strongly with the words of Saint Paul: *I have been crucified with Christ; yet I live, no longer I, but Christ lives in me; insofar as I now live in the flesh, I live by faith in the Son of God who has loved me and given himself up for me* (Gal 2:19b-20).

In his *Rule* we find many indications that Augustine was profoundly aware of the weakness of the flesh and the spirit even among those dedicated to the service of the Church, and that they were subject to many subtle temptations. Although as sinners we have been redeemed by the blood of Jesus, we remain in constant struggle with the forces of evil. We need support and correction from those with whom we share the Christian faith, guided by the Church, and strengthened by the grace of the sacraments that have been entrusted to her. In chapter one, number eight, Augustine sums up the life of those who follow Christ: "You are all to live together, therefore, *one in mind and one in heart* (cf. Ac 4:32), and honor God in one another, because *each of you has become His temple* (2 Cor 6:16)."

The Church owes to Augustine the doctrinal and moral foundation of religious life. We see his influence in every subsequent form that developed through the centuries. His writings on what constitutes holiness, union with God, were directed mostly to monks and other religious, those who had vowed the Gospel counsels of poverty, chastity, and obedience by living in a community dedicated to the service of the

Church. However, what he accomplished was to make everyone understand that the Christian life itself was a union with
God through Jesus. We are brought into the life of the Trinity through baptism because the Second Person, who became
one like us in all things but sin and redeemed us from sin,
has joined us to God. Augustine had taken the truths about
our redemption from Saint Paul and demonstrated to all —
bishop, priest, religious, and lay person alike — that we must
focus our lives on Christ, Son of God, crucified for us, if we
are to be one with the Triune God, which is the holiness to
which we are called.

A century later we find **Benedict** writing a *Rule* for his
monks, a *Rule* that would in time influence the purpose and
practices of monasticism throughout western Europe. It covered the use of food, clothing, sleep, work, the welcoming and
treatment of guests to the monastery, etc. He borrowed from
the monastic traditions of the East, especially the *Rule of St.
Basil,* but he gave it a more moderate tone. Ever prudent,
Benedict allowed for necessary adjustments in view of personal
circumstances and local conditions. There are regulations
concerning the responsibilities of the monks to each other,
the admission of new members, and how the monks shall relate to their own families as well as to those who live outside
the monastery. Special emphasis is placed on the monk's life
of prayer, which as their most important duty is called "the
work of God."

We see immediately that Benedict had a different intent
than Augustine. The monks stayed in one place, attached to
a specific monastery by a vow of stability. Their lives were not
primarily apostolic. They were dedicated to a complete and
uncompromising search for God and lived as faithful disciples
of Jesus, who was the ever obedient Son of His heavenly Father. When He prayed and when He worked, Christ honored
the Father who had sent Him. The monks looked to their
abbot as their guide in their common endeavor, and hoped
for his strong example. This perspective of Benedict is most

apparent when we read what he has to say in his *Rule For Monasteries* about the role of the community's superior, called the abbot (*Abba*), who is the father of the monastery and to whom the monks owe obedience as sons. They are to obey the abbot in all things, both in the temporal and the spiritual orders, in the same way that the disciples obeyed Jesus.

For the next six centuries the spiritual force that was dominant through many reforms and new foundations remained essentially what the Church had received from Augustine and Benedict. Through times of corruption that permeated even religious institutions, clergy and laity sought holiness of life in accord with the methods exemplified by monks and canons. The Church's liturgy, her ecclesiastical architecture, and her practices of devotion reflected the glory that belonged to God.

The Blurred Image of Jesus

By the 13th century, however, the Church's internal structures had become too weak to undertake with any effectiveness the needed reforms of clerical life and practices. The clergy were tied into feudal loyalties which fostered a spirit of compliance for the sake of survival. Both monasteries and cathedral chapters of Canons Regular depended on the benevolence of secular rulers for stability. Land control became the basis for effective spiritual power. The dignity of monks and clergy was compromised by the need to court favor with those who possessed wealth, in order to retain the endowments on which they lived. The scandalous lives of many whose duty it was to preach the Gospel created a climate of rebellion against Church authority on all levels. Something new was evidently called for. In the efforts made in many places to induce reform, ordinarily by laymen, the clergy were ridiculed, the sacraments neglected, and Church authority was ignored.

The climate was perfect for the revival of the ancient

Manichean heresy, now promoted by the Albigensians whose center was Albi in France. They believed that the world was inhabited by the two principles of good and evil, spiritual reality versus the material world. Christ was only a man who was subject to the forces of evil. There was no need for the Church since there had been no redemption. Others would not go that far, but denied the spiritual power of any cleric whose life did not reflect the poor and chaste Christ. These latter, known as Waldensians after their founder Peter Waldo of Lyons, lived poorly and demanded that all clergy do likewise. Soon they were denying everything fundamental to the Church's nature and mission, such as the Sacrifice of the Mass, the priesthood, and the resurrection of the body. They went about preaching with the Bible as their sole authority, and so have been called the forerunners of Protestantism. Nothing the popes tried, even a crusade into southern France, was successful against the rising tide of heresy and the rupture of the Church's unity with the consequent loss of souls.

Into this milieu came Dominic and Francis, whose friars would constitute the Church's most powerful force in their two-pronged assault on the sickness that had overwhelmed Christendom.

Dominic, anchored in the secure life of a Canon Regular in Spain, was shaken when he undertook a trip through France to Italy in 1203. He saw first-hand the havoc being wrought on the Church by the Albigensians. The spirituality that he eventually developed was a response to an apostolic need. He was already formed in the way of Saint Augustine, and dedicated to the service of the Church. Now he would advance in that tradition, but bring to it a different focus. He had set out with a band of preachers into southern France to combat heresy by energetic scriptural preaching that emanated from a lifestyle unencumbered by property or by obligations to any local interest. His concern would be the good of the universal Church.

He readily saw that the image of Christ — true God and

true Man — had been lost to many. The evident moral disorder that existed among many powerful people, which included ecclesiastics, made it difficult to see the presence of Jesus in the Church. Thus Dominic developed an itinerant manner of living that emulated the poverty of the self-styled reformers who were claiming that the Church had abandoned the poor and humble Christ. The charges were well-founded and received much attention among the ranks of the poor. Dominic also viewed a life of mortification and prayer as necessary preparation for one who would proclaim the cross of Jesus as the source of grace. Jesus and the Church must be seen as one.

Dominic knew that he must join his Master in this incarnate foolishness if the Truth was to be accepted. The eternal Wisdom of God had lived among His people as truly one of them. He was subject to all human joys and sorrows, to pain and weariness. All this was because He had come to redeem His people from their sins, by offering Himself in sacrifice as priest and victim. Dominic respected the logic of the worldly wise. They expect that a disciple of a crucified Lord ought to live that which he preaches.

What Dominic did was to reorder his life with a different thrust. He would take the Jesus as spoken of by Augustine, namely, the eternal Word of God whose dignity we all share by reason of our baptism, and put the focus more on His human nature which made Him one of us. As true Man He was able to redeem us from sin by His death and to give us the promise of eternal life by His resurrection. He lived as we do and thereby became the mediator between God and man. The people, of which He was part, having been redeemed by His blood and baptized into His death and resurrection, have become a priestly people because of Him. Thus all the elements of the spirituality we have from Saint Dominic focus on Jesus as priest. Followers of Dominic go about preaching and teaching as Jesus their Master did; they offer sacrifice for sin by lives of mortification and reparation as they travel; they live simply as Jesus and His disciples did; and they pray with the

Church as the Body of Christ. Each person following the way of Dominic, whether cleric or lay, married or single, must always act as a priestly person, united with Jesus the priest, whose life was given for His people.

During this same period, the first quarter of the 13th century, we find **Francis** of Assisi responding to circumstances in his personal life and not to conditions in the Church. His first years of conversion, from 1206 to 1208, he spent living a hermit's life as one of the poor. He began to know Jesus in manual labor (e.g., restoring run-down wayside churches) and in begging for food and shelter when the recompense for his labor was insufficient to sustain him. He found his inspiration in the Gospels, overwhelmed as he was that the Son of God lived such a simple life on earth, indeed was born in poverty and worked with His hands. His example of humility, to serve and not to be served, brought Francis to the realization that Jesus had become totally one with those whom He had come to redeem from their sins. He had become in fact a brother to them, sharing all aspects of their lives. From Him they learned all that the Father wanted them to know. He said: *Take my yoke upon you and learn from me, for I am meek and humble of heart; and you will find rest for yourselves* (Mt 11:29).

When Francis began to attract others who wished to live as he did, he taught them to seek from the Gospels the example of Jesus who had gone that way before them. They were to preach penance, of vices and virtues, "in few and simple words." They were to call the people to a true conversion of heart that flows from the love of Jesus and demands that we love all as brothers and sisters of Jesus. We must be good to them, always forgiving, never judging, and be obedient to those He has given us for guidance in His Holy Church.

Francis gave us a broader understanding of Jesus as our brother. We were not just brothers and sisters to those who were children of God by baptism, but to all who were made to the image of God, including "Saracens and other infidels." And that respect is owed to all who are united as family, because Christ, walking the same earth and breathing the same air, made all creatures brothers and sisters to Himself and therefore to us. No one before Francis would have thought to say: Brother Sun, Sister Moon, Brothers Fire, Wind, and Air, Sisters Water, Death, and Earth our mother. His concern for animals was not only because they were creatures of God and thus reflected His glory. But it was also Brother Wolf and Sister Lark and even Sister Worm because the Son of God by His incarnation became brother to them all.

Francis showed to the Church the true Jesus of whom the Gospels speak, that His being true Man means that He really lived as we do. The man from Assisi could rejoice in the privilege to live the same human life as the Son of the Eternal Father. This example benefited especially the average people, who were often illiterate and could only appreciate what they witnessed. But it also had a most beneficial effect on merchants, noblemen, and clergy who came to see the Son of God in Francis and his friars through the example of their poor and humble lives.

As we see, Dominic and Francis both focused the attention of the Church on the humanity of Christ: one on Jesus the priest, whose total life was a sacrifice; and the other on Jesus our brother, who shared our human condition. Each showed the laity, both learned and unschooled, what was demanded of a Christian, namely, to live as Jesus did. Both Dominican and Franciscan friars, each with a different thrust and style, brought new holiness to the Church and a return to the Christ-like attitude among the worldly-minded clergy themselves. Their ranks had grown by tremendous numbers, as Innocent III had hoped, and through them the reforms of Innocent reached their fulfillment in the Council of Lyons in 1274, where the influence of two Dominicans (Saints Albert the Great and Thomas Aquinas) and a Franciscan (Saint Bonaventure) was greatly felt. By 1288 a Franciscan friar became Pope, Nicholas IV.

Confusion Reigns

We now move ahead three centuries to the time of the Protestant revolution and the Council of Trent, not too long after the opening of the Americas. The Church had been under direct attack since 1517 with Martin Luther's challenge, and by 1545 she was well divided. New Christian churches had been formed, taking from the Church of Rome whatever suited them. There was need to come to her defense, to bring to the new lands the message of the Gospel, and to repair the damage to her holiness with a healing spirit. Emerging on the scene, sent by God, we have Ignatius and Teresa, one behind the other. What vision of Jesus were they to offer us?

Ignatius thought like the soldier he was. He saw the Faith under siege from forces on many fronts, and he felt the call to give his life in its defense. He also saw opportunities for new endeavors, to bring the Gospel to new lands. But first intense preparation was needed. In the first place there was spiritual fitness. In his *Exercises* we find their purpose stated: to help anyone who used them "to conquer himself and to regulate his life so that he will not be influenced in his decisions by any inordinate attachments." Intellectual weaponry and the skills needed to use it had to be acquired. For Ignatius this was done in Paris. Even to this day, Jesuits begin their training with the *Exercises*, and they are submitted to vigorous intellectual conditioning before being sent forth to defend the Church and promote her mission of salvation.

The Ignatian imagery of the "Two Standards" gives us our insight into his vision of the Church. "Christ our supreme Captain and Lord" has assembled on the plains of Jerusalem an army of apostles, disciples, etc., and "sends them throughout the whole world to spread His sacred doctrine." The enemy is Lucifer whose cohorts gather on the fields of Babylon and are also sent forth, but in his case "to ensnare men and to bind them in chains." The troops of Ignatius would struggle against ignorance of the Faith by supporting and establishing institutions of Christian learning; and they would venture into the lands of the newly discovered Americas and the newly opened Far East, and wherever else Christ was not known. All this would be done in loyalty and obedience to the Vicar of Christ on earth, under whose orders they would be sent.

In this period of ecclesiastical revolution the lines of defense were drawn. The Church reformed her methods for preparing candidates to the priesthood, and defined her doctrines clearly in the catechism issued from the Council of Trent. Yet the damage done by the Protestant reformers to her image as the divine instrument of salvation needed to be undone, and this would take not just words but strong example. The Society of Jesus, although most certainly not alone, led the way in the restoration of faith in the Church as the Body of Christ through whose sacraments we receive the fruits of redemption. There was also a need to return to a basic reality of the Christian Faith, namely, that all Christians are called not just to live a good moral life in hope of an eternal reward, but have been invited to a personal union of love with Jesus, that is, to holiness.

Such intimate oneness with the Son of God is intrinsically linked to the fulfillment of the responsibilities we have from God. However, God's will cannot be accepted and loved without constant communion with the source of grace, Jesus Himself. At the time of which we speak there were reforms occurring in many existing religious institutes, a return to simpler structures that gave emphasis to the contemplative dimension of religious life. Among these, of course, is the one with which **Teresa** of Avila played the key role. Through her writings, her personal experiences, and the story of her reform of the Carmelite Order, she has taught us more than any other about the true nature of prayer and how to prepare for this great gift. She has shown us that prayer calls for an openness to God that will give us the desire and strength to live by heroic standards. This will necessarily include suffering as an essential component of holiness. Like all the others who make up our *Great Six,* she pointed to the cross of Jesus as the source of power in lifting us from sin and into the embrace of God's love.

Teresa recounts the travails that came to her from inside and outside her community as she sought to return her Order to its pristine rule. She speaks of misunderstandings and persecutions. Her own frail health was a trial and the long trips necessary to establish new convents were difficult. Insufficient food, inadequate sleeping accommodations, and weather conditions often brought their share of misery. At times she felt the loss of consolation in prayer, which begot periods of discouragement. She often was tempted to discontinue her work of reform.

Yet she always kept in mind what her Savior had suffered for her. Uniting herself to Him, she asked that He make use of her sufferings to give the grace of conversion to others. She knew that Jesus gave us every opportunity to take up our cross and follow Him, to share His role as Redeemer. This called forth her great trust in the "dear Friend" who offered her the privilege to suffer with Him who had first suffered for her.

* * * *

The focus of our saints is always on Jesus, but not in the same way. With perhaps too much imagination I like to picture each of our saints back home, walking along the roadway with Jesus. A childhood friend comes along and an introduction is called for. In *Thagaste* it might be: "This is Jesus, my good friend. He has come from His Father in heaven and wants to take me back with Him." In *Nursia*: "This is Jesus, the Son of God, my Master. He has come from heaven to show me how to be a son of God also." In *Osma*: "This is Jesus, my Savior. He has come from heaven to teach me all He knows, and to die for my sins." In *Assisi*: "This is Jesus, my brother from heaven. He has come to live with me." Near the castle of *Loyola*: "This is Jesus, my Lord from heaven. He wants me to join in His work." And finally the most audacious of all in *Avila*: "This is Jesus my friend. He wants me to help Him redeem the world."

CHAPTER FOUR

SHOULD WE LOOK FOR A NEW JESUS?

T he social milieu in which we live today differs greatly from that of even the latest of our saints, Teresa. We have passed through the industrial revolution; transportation and communications have progressed in giant leaps since even a century ago. Sovereign nations have emerged from the era of colonialism; monarchies have fallen before the tide of democracy. The ability of man to destroy himself and his world is a constant threat. The Church herself has survived the age of Jansenism, Gallicanism, Rationalism, and the Enlightenment. She has lost all her temporal power, except over a small Vatican City. In this century she has encountered Modernism, and still struggles with the influence of existentialism and its corollary, relativism. Anti-clericalism continues in the three so-called Catholic countries of France, Spain, and Italy. Increasingly destructive war is still part of the world in which political forces contend, sometimes in the name of religion.

Are the ways of Augustine and Benedict, Dominic and Francis, Ignatius and Teresa relevant in our day as instruments for reform? There is no reason that they should not be, for the conditions of today are not essentially different from those in any generation. There will always be good struggling with evil, truth with error, sanctity with sinfulness. The Church is made up of sinners, whose lives often appear no different from those of their fellow citizens. The situation is exasperated when the clergy appear to be taken up more with material or social

concerns than with their role as spiritual guides and media-
tors between God and man.

The Church has always had to struggle against becoming the victim of political or social circumstances. In the time
of Augustine and Benedict she needed to separate herself
from the Roman structure of empire and its excesses; Dominic
and Francis helped extricate her from the restraints of the
feudal system; Ignatius and Teresa found the Church caught
in the search for national identities. In each era the goals of
many reformers were admirable, seeking to return to the simplicity of the Gospel, but the solutions often called for a
change in the fundamental nature of the Church. The real
need was to seek reform of the human structures she had
molded, structures which no longer served her purpose as an
instrument of salvation, as the beacon of truth, or as the minister of God's mercy.

Much like the individual Christian, the Church is in continuing need of conversion. Indeed today she has been called
to a substantial renewal by the Second Vatican Council. Although we may be well on the way, we still await the fulfillment
of that hope. We have not made the world fully aware of the
person of Jesus, true God and true Man, who redeemed us
from sin, rose from the dead to give us hope of eternal life in
His Kingdom, and whose mission of salvation is the work of
the Catholic Church. The problem remains that we still have
not inspired many of our own to repentance. In order that
Jesus might increase, be more clearly seen in the lives of His
followers, we must decrease the human failings among us that
turn good people away from Him.

So we ask: to accomplish this must we wait for two more
saints to be raised up in the Church to show us new ways of
spirituality that best fit our own time? In the first place, I do
not think we can wait; nor do I think that we need to. Those
spiritualities which have stood the test of time need to be re-
vitalized by those who profess them. My hope is that this short
work will make a contribution toward that end: to help bring

the charism of Augustine and Benedict, Dominic and Francis, Ignatius and Teresa into play as we of the various spirituality traditions struggle with our identity in the modern world.

When society seems to be out of control with wars, economic disasters, social pathologies, cultural clashes, etc., good Christians become concerned with the moral instability produced by such upheavals. They sense that the Church is having little impact on people's lives, or even that the Gospel itself has failed. The Church's enemies, often abetted by her own, cast doubts on the sincerity of our ecclesiastical leaders. When they insist on the moral teaching of Christ, the suggestion is made that they are more interested in preserving control than in spreading the compassion of Jesus.

In 1962 Pope John XXIII sensed that the moral influence of the Church was waning, and he saw the need to put a new face on Catholicism that sincere men and women would respect. He wanted us to strengthen the spiritual force of Christ's love that had been weakened by outmoded practices and attitudes. He called us to conversion through the Second Vatican Council. A plan of renewal was outlined in the area of worship, the pastoral office of bishops, the formation and ministry of priests, religious life, relation to non-Catholic religions, and the responsibilities of the laity in the mission of the Church. To make sure that reform did not remove what was fundamental and unchangeable, the Council expressed the essential nature of the Church as instituted by Christ in the *Dogmatic Constitution on the Church.* This document (in Latin: *Lumen Gentium*) almost demands that it be read every year by anyone working seriously on renewal. To be especially noted is the final paragraph of chapter one: *The Mystery of the Church.* It reads:

> The Church, "like a stranger in a foreign land, presses forward amid the persecutions of the world and the consolation of God," (St. Augustine) announcing the cross and death of the Lord until he comes (1 Cor 11:26). But

> by the power of the risen Lord she is given strength to
> overcome, in patience and in love, her sorrows, and her
> difficulties, both those that are from within and those that
> are from without, so that she may reveal in the world,
> faithfully, however darkly, the mystery of her Lord until,
> in the consummation, it shall be manifested in full light.

Many good things have happened in the life of the
Church since 1965, when the Council closed with great expectations. A beginning has been made in several areas, from liturgical reform to ecumenism. The laity have been empowered
on many levels to participate in the Church's mission. Yet we
still await the great revival of charity and holiness that we were
hoping for. Some would claim that we changed too much too
fast. Others feel that we are going too slowly and have not
changed enough. I suspect that the latter is true. Of course,
that depends on what kind of change one is looking for.

Some Pitfalls to Avoid

In every period of Church history, when change was obviously
a need, there have always been impetuous and impatient reformers, although well-intentioned, who often led people away
from the Truth. What has happened in the past cannot be
ignored. Our attempts to make the Church more relevant and
effective in our modern world must be passed through the
prism of experience. We have been this way before. We must
watch that the same errors do not return with new names.

Let us make a quick review of the past, since the basic
problem has been and remains our sinfulness. Augustine
struggled with it in his own life. He sought to reconcile the
contradiction between the good he hoped for and the evil he
did. First he accepted the Manichean belief in the two disparate principles of good and evil, darkness and light. Eventually
he found his answer in the doctrine of redemption as ex-

pressed in the letters of Saint Paul, namely, that Jesus Christ, true God and true Man, had conquered sin and death by His death and resurrection. Through baptism we share in the life of God, one with the Father and the Spirit through the Son made Man, who redeemed us from sin and by whose grace we are able to rise from our sinfulness. This takes place within the Catholic Church through the Mass and the Sacraments, and with the cooperation of those who seek the grace and salvation which they confer.

Within the Christian community itself, however, Augustine found those who would not accept the mystery of redemption as revealed in the Scriptures. Possibly they felt that it was not working, that Christians often did not seem different from their pagan neighbors. More probably, like Arius, they were not able to reconcile in faith the union of a divine person (light) with the corruption of human nature (darkness). Jesus could not be God. Others, like Nestorius, did not deny the Trinity of Persons in God, but claimed that Jesus was a distinct human person with the consequent moral limitations. Others, like Pelagius, denied that Adam's sin was passed on to us, and therefore redemption by the Son of God was unnecessary. Salvation was possible by the force of one's own will, strengthened by the example we have from Jesus.

Lack of faith in the Blessed Trinity and in the Second Person as truly having become Man had begun to undermine the Church's very foundation. Doubt was cast on the Church as having a divine origin, and in the priesthood as a share in the divine power, and in the Mass as the memorial of the redemptive act of a divine Person, and in the Eucharist as the true presence of Jesus in our midst. Consequently, for many the Church became a mere human institution that could go astray; the sacraments were mere rituals or symbols. Priests have no special dignity apart from their own goodness and learning.

The process was often reversed. Because pope or bishop

was perceived to have betrayed Christ, they need not be obeyed. If a priest was known to have sinned grievously, any Mass which he offered or any sacrament he administered had no power to confer grace (Donatism). Questions about sacramental validity became doubts about the Church as the Body of Christ and eventually about Jesus as truly God.

This became evident again in the twelfth century. The new Manicheans were the Albigensians, who saw that Christ had been compromised by His own. They reacted to the power struggles between hierarchy and nobility, and to the comfortable and the immoral lives of some clergy, by rejecting the authority of the Church, her priesthood, and her sacraments. They proclaimed that, since the Church had allowed sin to overcome her institutions, she must give way to something new. The reformers would go back to the Scriptures and begin again. Dominic and his preachers came to the defense of the truth and showed the way for a renewal of the moral life expected of Christians.

Strengthened by mortified, prayerful and poor lives, the Dominicans showed that to use such reasoning for rejecting the Church is to say that Jesus did not keep His promise to remain with her until the end of the world. This would imply that He could not make such a promise because He was not really God. Nor could He give a divine command to teach and sanctify. And since the Church had gone astray, the Spirit must no longer be dwelling within her. Dominic, however, made it clear that the Church is the presence of Jesus in the world even when He appears bloody and sometimes unrecognizable, just as He did when He hung upon the cross.

The same heresies would surface again four hundred years later, but in a different context. By the sixteenth century a developing spirit of nationalism was dividing the Christian peoples. The pope's temporal power was being challenged, and this carried over into the spiritual realm. It was especially hard to distinguish between the two. There was obvious need for a reformation of the Church's institutions which appeared not to represent the poor and humble Jesus very well. This opened questions about the nature of the Church and the mission of Jesus. In the teachings of Luther and Calvin the philosophical analysis of good versus evil (*a la* Manicheism) became a debate over redemption, salvation, faith and grace.

What remained was the Scriptures and the example of Jesus, who perhaps was or perhaps was not the Son of God. The kingdom of heaven that He spoke about was within. The Church's hierarchical organization had been built by men. Christians were free to organize themselves as they willed. Any persons chosen to lead the baptized received their right to govern from the people themselves. The authority of the pope and bishops was either rejected outright, or (as decreed by Henry VIII of England) was subject to that of the king. Except for the Church of England, the reformers for the most part declared that the only necessary sacrament was baptism. Even those who accepted the Eucharist, very evidently contained in the Scriptures, considered it a commemorative meal which united the community of believers by a sharing of the body and blood of Jesus (real or symbolic). It was not a sacrifice; hence no need for priests.

So much for reform. The present state of Protestantism, with its constant splintering down to a simple fundamentalism, speaks for itself.

How could this happen in a western Europe that, at least in name, shared the faith of Rome? With tensions between various ethnic groups confusing every issue, the vast majority of Christians before 1545 were finding it difficult to make distinctions between the Church's teachings and the actions of her ministers. In looking to meet the new social challenges to her unity, the Church recognized that the principal reason for the success of protesting reformers was the ignorance of the faith among the faithful and the inadequate preparation of priests as teachers. This concern, as well as the need for renewal of form and spirit in her institutions, became the driving force in the Council of Trent. Liturgical and catechetical reform and a new program for the training of priests headed the list of priorities. Ignatius and his followers joined the first line of defense in education and evangelization and their success became an example for others to follow. New religious congregations were founded in response to particular needs of charity and/or education for the poor, and the older orders began to take on new vigor. Renewal had set in.

What Is the Situation Today?

A marked similarity exists between the pre-Trent and the post-Vatican II generations. A changed society since 1545 makes for many differences, but the situation within the Church now reflects many of the same problems that faced us then. Today a deep ignorance of the fundamentals of the faith can be found even among the most educated, which is aggravated by a high level of sophistication. Personalism and materialism have replaced national self-interest. The "institutional" Church is seen as an obstacle to individual freedom. As Manicheism influenced former ages, relativism has become the philosophical basis for much modern religious thought. In effect, our age has reached a compromise between good and evil.

Many have accepted the premise that our physical nature is neither good nor evil and has no need for redemption. Since our spiritual nature always chooses what is good for us, we are able to effect our own salvation (*a la* Pelagianism). The only evil is to interfere with another person's freedom. Tolerance is the universal virtue. To defend an absolute truth about creation, human nature, or our relationship to the Creator is to seek control over others. So much for a Church which is based on revealed Truth that has come from above and not from within.

As has happened so often in the past, some who want to bring a new spirit among the baptized are not adverse to changing the nature of the Church as we have understood her from the beginning. There is a call for a "new reformation" because we live in an enlightened world. We must accept a few compromises. Some of those proposed are: (a) All religions possess truth since the religious impulse comes from our nature; hence ecumenism must seek for oneness in common goals. (b) Christ, the source of grace, calls us to be one; hence the community should determine the rituals which best express this purpose. (c) All persons are equal before God; hence all the baptized share in His eternal priesthood. (d) We are obliged to act in accord with what we perceive to be best for ourselves and others; hence morality is determined by intention. (e) Leaders are raised up from the baptized by reason of their learning and holiness; hence the pope and bishops merit our obedience insofar as they respond to the Holy Spirit who resides in the entire Church.

The Church, however, professes that she exists by the will of Jesus Christ, true God and true Man. She keeps in mind His words to the Apostles as He prepared to ascend to the Father after His resurrection from the dead: *All power in heaven and on earth has been given to me. Go, therefore, and make disciples of all nations, baptizing them in the name of the Father, and of the Son, and of the Holy Spirit, teaching them to observe all that I have commanded you. And behold I am with you always, until the end of the age* (Mt 28:18b-20). Her central mission remains the same: to bring to all the saving grace of redemption from sin and the promise of eternal life, that came about by the death of Jesus on the cross and His rising from the dead. We celebrate the Eucharistic Sacrifice as the memorial of this great mystery. The pope and bishops, as successors of Peter and the Apostles, protect this heritage from any variance.

Yet even those who accept the Catholic Church as the presence of Jesus in this world can be influenced, however subtly, by the tenets of religious relativism. How explain the deemphasis on the Mass as a sacrifice (though never denied) and the stress that we assemble for a "sacred meal" as a people of God and a community of faith. Some would suggest that this is the cause of a growing irreverence toward the Blessed Sacrament. We do know that an increasing number of our co-religionists are questioning the Real Presence of Jesus in the Eucharist. More and more people want priests to be "regular guys." Less are accepting the pope's pronouncements as the last word. Bishops, successors to the Apostles, are looked upon as administrators rather than stewards of the mysteries of faith, and they are judged accordingly. The sacrament of reconciliation has fallen into disuse, as if sin no longer existed. These examples raise a warning for us to be careful in our desire for renewal. We cannot let a spirit of discontent with Church leaders distract us from the all-important focus for each of us: what does Jesus expect of me?

Renewal and Holiness Go Hand in Hand

The primary concern of all must be to respond to the Father's love for us. This places upon us a personal responsibility to fulfill His will in the particular circumstances in which He has placed us. We know His will through Jesus the Son, and in union with all the baptized, made one by the Holy Spirit who guides the Church. We help bring about this unity by the proper use of the talents and opportunities which we receive, whether we touch only a few of our brothers and sisters in Jesus, or reach thousands. Our call is to build up the Body of Christ and contribute by our holiness to the fulfillment of her mission.

In our struggles to renew the Church in our age according to the spirit of the Second Vatican Council, we must keep constantly in mind some very basic principles which we all know, but in our impatience sometimes forget. These are: (1) the Holy Spirit is the author of renewal; (2) our efforts must be actions of faith if we expect to succeed; (3) we must trust in God's promises to His people or we will be frustrated; and (4) our motivation must be love, the sacrifice of our own wills, or we risk destruction.

One thing that we must be clear about is our special relationship to Jesus Himself. This will keep us focused on the particular area to which we have been assigned by the Holy Spirit. We cannot go in every direction, but we can pursue our designated course. How well we do will depend on the particular attitude we take toward Jesus as our Lord. Therefore, let us return briefly to our six saints. None of them was involved in every aspect of Church life. But each was well focused on his/her own special purpose.

The renewal in the life of the Church during the turbulent years of which we have spoken (5th, 13th, and 16th centuries) took place on many fronts. Our saints did not even initiate Church renewal. Their followers became the instruments of reform that had already begun in the hearts of countless individuals and which the Church herself put in motion by official actions. We need only review the history of the various ecumenical councils, especially Nicaea (325), IV Lateran (1215), and Trent (1545). In these times each saint brought into play the power of a particular spiritual vision, which gave success to reforms already begun. They became beacons of light to guide others in the work of regeneration. Their influence through those who followed their example permeated the Church with new spiritual vigor. This led to the change that was needed in personal lives and in the style and form of Church institutions. Changes were made by those who had the power to make them, namely, popes, bishops, priests, scholars, civic leaders, etc. The whole of society was the beneficiary of renewed efforts in education and in missionary activity.

Augustine, Dominic, and Ignatius spurred the defense

against heresies that had diluted the Faith, efforts which were
made effective by the special forms of their unique spiritual
strategies. On the other hand Benedict, Francis, and Teresa
drew people back to God in a more subtle manner because
their special ways concerned lifestyle. They followed the ad-
age that actions speak louder than words. Monks reminded
us that we must give our lives totally to God. Franciscans exemplified the poverty and humility of Jesus to remind us that
all who act in His name must be servants to their brothers and
sisters. Carmelites showed us that a life of contemplative prayer
was fundamental to any work of reformation.

In this sense we speak of the Augustinians, Dominicans,
and Jesuits as apostolic orders, whose spirituality motivates the
work to which they have been called. Benedictines,
Franciscans, and Carmelites reverse the perspective. Their call
is to demonstrate special ways to live the Gospel, and this de-
termines what need they will respond to or at least the form
their work will take. For each saint, then, it is a matter of spe-
cialization.

We have the right to ask to what extent the various spiritualities of which we speak have influenced the progress of
renewal in our Vatican II Church. It is impossible, of course,
to judge accurately. I believe that it can be safely said, however, that the hope of the Council would already be realized
if all the religious congregations, secular orders, and secular
institutes which embody in various forms the spiritualities of
our six saints had renewed themselves early on. We know that
this had not happened. Most are still struggling to establish
their respective identities. Some individual members are even
causing difficulties within the Church community. Yet it would
be fair to say that most religious who have remained with their
congregations, orders, or institutes have been working at renewal within their ranks, so as to be of service to the People
of God. The heart of the matter in this effort has been declared
in paragraph 2b of the Second Vatican Council's *Decree on the*

Up-to-date Renewal of Religious Life (in Latin: *Perfectae Caritatis*). It states succinctly: "The spirit and aims of each founder should be faithfully accepted and retained."

One major problem in this regard is that so many religious cannot seem to differentiate, except in some external characteristics, the precise charism of their founder in contrast with that of all the others. The basic principles of the spirituality which they profess are generally known. These principles get lost, however, in the translation to practical life. In the eyes of many among the laity and secular clergy, religious appear to be all the same, often do the same works, and live a rather secure and comfortable life.

Be that as it may, I would like to share my own understanding of the basic six spiritualities so as to be a help where help might be needed. I will not confine myself to the forms lived by religious, but will address the spiritualities themselves as gifts to the Church for both clergy and laity, married and single, men and women, young and old. I believe that we find the answer to Church renewal for our generation within the spirit of Augustine and Benedict, Dominic and Francis, Ignatius and Teresa. They have found varying expressions through the centuries, and perhaps new forms are needed to meet today's circumstances. For them to be effective, however, I also believe that for application today each spirituality must be trimmed to its essence and the appropriate focus be made on a specific area of Church life as we, the People of God, face the modern world.

EVERYBODY CAN BE HOLY

O ne idea that the Second Vatican Council laid to rest was the opinion too often expressed by some among the laity that anyone called to become a saint would have a vocation to the priesthood or to religious life. Chapter Five of the *Dogmatic Constitution on the Church*, entitled *The Call to Holiness*, re-affirmed what the Church has always taught. "It is therefore quite clear that all Christians in any state or walk of life are called to the fullness of Christian life and to the perfection of love, and by this holiness a more human manner of life is fostered also in earthly society." We might take the latter phrase as a call to the laity that their holiness is especially needed to bring Gospel principles into secular affairs.

This is why we need to make certain that there is no doubt in anyone's mind that the *Great Six*, as I call them, were raised up to guide along the path to holiness not only their own followers, but also every generous soul who loves God. The validity of each spirituality has been confirmed over and over by many popes. True, each saint was a priest and/or religious. They lived specific forms of consecrated life. The principles they espoused, however, came from the Gospels, and so are applicable to every Christian man and woman, whether married or single. History confirms that the laity have always seen our saints as models of holiness for themselves too. In fact, there is a secular component of the Orders which embody each spirituality. Although known in the past by different names, they are now called: Augustinian Seculars, Benedictine Oblates, Dominican Laity, Secular Franciscans, Christian Life Communities (Ignatian), and Secular Carmelites.

Thus we accept the understanding that the six distinct spiritualities are available to everyone. Each spirituality, however, does have a distinctive appeal to different persons. The task at hand is to differentiate our saints so that their ways to holiness can be seen as separate choices for lay persons of every "state or walk of life."

Our saints were consecrated by vow to the fulfillment of the Church's mission. To this end they joined themselves in a community with others of like mind. This choice was made as a special call from God and confirmed by the Church. We affirm, nonetheless, that no one attains holiness in a vacuum — whether that person be lay, cleric or religious. From birth all human persons are associated with others for survival and for the accomplishment of some work. Our lives always intermingle with that of others. It may be the same person or persons much of the time, or different groups of persons at different times for different purposes. Society itself is made up of interrelated groups of persons who are connected by civil or social concerns. The question is: will we employ our personal involvement with others as a human necessity or as a means to holiness? To make them an effective means to union with God depends on the way such contacts become an extension of our own very personal relationship to Jesus.

Whether we are relating to members of our immediate family, or to those with whom we work to make a living, or to associates in civic organizations and charitable endeavors, or to members of our parish family, etc., we are called to love them as we love ourselves. This requires that we accept them as they are, to be patient with them when their ways are irritating, to forgive them when they take advantage of us, and to cooperate with them in our common effort. To treat them

as Jesus expects us to do demands that we do not place ourselves in contention or in competition with them. The *community life* of which we are part must be utilized as a means to
holiness, and not to be tolerated merely because we need each
other. Rather, we should embrace this need as essential to
acquire the humility which is the foundation of all virtue and
the prerequisite for sanctity. *I give you a new commandment: love
one another. As I have loved you, so you also should love one another*
(Jn 13:34).

To make our *community life* more than a social need, but
a spiritual adventure, we must ask ourselves how we perceive
each person with whom we live and/or work in the varied aspects of mutual dependency. Life requires that we give of
ourselves in order to fulfill the purpose of the common effort.
To do so without measure demands that we overcome our own
selfish interests. We must frequently deal with the disquietude
within that is the effect of the perceived lack of generosity in
others. We struggle against false judgments and thoughts of
retaliation when offended. Yet it is possible to transform our
personal relationship with Jesus into a bond with others that
would express our conviction that Jesus loves the other members of our "community" because He died for them too.

The way that we relate to others is influenced by many
factors, including age, experiences, personality, etc. Some
persons attract us by their goodness or general "niceness" and
others repel us because of some type of boorish or conde-
scending behavior. Toward many more, perhaps, we are totally neutral. Yet we are commanded by Jesus to love all as He
loves all, and this calls for more than an attitude of toleration.
True love requires positive acts of charity. That is the challenge
that, when accepted, opens the way to a close union with the
Triune God through the Son made Man. This is the holiness
which we pursue.

Our Saints Show the Way

A strong spiritual motivation is required in order to stay focused on our goal. We are too easily distracted by the variety of circumstances that surround each relationship, even at different times with the same persons. The six spiritualities provide a focus that appeals to a very personal perspective on the Christian life, namely, our own relationship to Jesus. We cannot say it often enough. Each spirituality must center on Jesus. He is the object of our affection, and He unites us to the Father and the Holy Spirit. *All things have been handed over to me by my Father. No one knows the Son except the Father, and no one knows the Father except the Son and anyone to whom the Son wishes to reveal Him* (Mt 11:27). *When the Advocate comes whom I will send you from the Father, the Spirit of truth that proceeds from the Father, He will testify to me* (Jn 15:26).

In this world we all live by faith, and that includes everyone of every condition, namely, workers and scholars, parents and children, religious and priests, popes and bishops. Our knowledge of Jesus grows through faith. Only then can we be confident that He can be trusted. Thus we grow in a relationship of love that makes us ready to do whatever He asks of us, no matter how difficult or seemingly unreasonable. This becomes the force of our love for everyone else who shares our faith. When Augustine spoke to his priests, Benedict to his monks, Dominic to his preachers, Francis to his brothers, Ignatius to his companions and Teresa to her nuns, they spoke about Jesus as they knew Him — primarily from the Gospels. Their words transcend any particular place or time or circumstance and can readily be applied to each of us today.

Our understanding of Jesus grows in accord with the way we speak to Him in prayer. And our love deepens as we share His life in accord with our own special circumstances. The proving ground is the form of life we share with others — religious or secular — that affords the opportunities to love those with whom God has joined us. How we relate to all these persons will depend on our personal relationship to Jesus.

If, like Augustine, we see Jesus as a *Friend*, we will treat others too as friends of Jesus. Augustine considered each person as a wonder of God's creative love, even in a sometimes imperfect and sinful condition. He saw himself as part of everyone else's struggle — grace overcoming sin — because Jesus had died for all others too. His love for them requires that they receive our love and respect as well. *But I say to you, love your enemies, and pray for those who persecute you, that you may be children of your heavenly Father, for He makes His sun rise on the bad and the good, and causes rain to fall on the just and the unjust.... So be perfect, just as your heavenly Father is perfect* (Mt 5:44-45, 48).

If, like Benedict, we see Jesus as our *Master*, and recognize ourselves as His disciples and as adopted children of His heavenly Father, we will view others also as sons and daughters of God. Benedict taught us to seek union with God, who is patient with others as He is merciful to us. We are members of the same family of God, made so by Jesus, His Son who became Man. *Someone told Him, "Your mother and your brothers are standing outside, asking to speak with you." But He said in reply to the one who told Him, "Who is my mother? Who are my brothers?" And stretching out His hand toward His disciples, He said, "Here are my mother and my brothers. For whoever does the will of my heavenly Father is brother, and sister, and mother to me"* (Mt 12:47-50).

If, like Dominic, we see Jesus as the *Savior* who offered Himself for our salvation, we will accept others also as equal recipients of Christ's redemptive death on the cross as we are ourselves. Dominic would have us be patient and understanding with those who are in error because of ignorance. He knew that men and women of good will would be receptive to the truth when taught by those who treated them with respect and showed them the simple life of Jesus who is our way, our truth, and our life. *Come to me, all you who labor and are burdened, and I will give you rest. Take my yoke upon you and learn from me, for I*

am meek and humble of heart; and you will find rest for yourselves.
For my yoke is easy and my burden light (Mt 11:28-30).

If, like Francis, we see Jesus as our *Brother*, we will accept
others as brothers or sisters of Jesus and will treat them accordingly. Francis was totally amazed that the Son of God had become Man, who shared our labors and our family joys, our
disappointments and our need for friendship. He, king of all
creation, was born in poverty and, although master and
teacher, washed the feet of His apostles. He became our servant and died in humiliation and suffering. As brother to us
all in our human condition, Jesus challenges us: *As I have loved*
you, so you also should love one another (Jn 13:34).

If, like Ignatius, we see Jesus as the *Lord* whom we serve
in His mission of salvation, we will look upon others as called
to share the compassion of Jesus and to participate in His work.
To Ignatius each person was someone to whom Jesus was showing the way to eternal life, and as a companion of Jesus he had
a responsibility to lead by good example and sound teaching,
supported by acts of charity. *At the sight of the crowds, His heart*
was moved with pity for them because they were troubled and aban-
doned, like sheep without a shepherd. Then He said to His disciples,
"The harvest is abundant but the laborers are few; so ask the master
of the harvest to send out laborers for his harvest" (Mt 9:36-38).

If, like Teresa, we see Jesus as our *Redeemer*, who suffered
for us, we will look upon others as friends with whom we are
united in His Passion. Teresa saw herself as a partner in the
redemptive work of Jesus, who died for all. She offered herself and all her suffering, work, and personal difficulties as a
sharing in the sacrifice of Jesus Himself. She would demonstrate the saving power of love to all with whom she lived and
worked by seeking only the good of others in total abandonment of her own will. *Whoever loves father or mother more than me*
is not worthy of me, and whoever loves son or daughter more than me
is not worthy of me; and whoever does not take up his cross and fol-
low me is not worthy of me. Whoever finds his life will lose it, and
whoever loses his life for my sake will find it (Mt 10:37-39).

We Have Just Begun

Our basic purpose is to compare the spirituality traditions of the *Great Six* whose legacies have defined the holiness of the Church through the centuries and whose influence continues in the lives of countless men and women today. By such comparison we hope to understand the distinct genius of each. We have reviewed their origins, the effect of their respective historical eras on the choices they made, their attitude towards those with whom they lived and worked, and the very specific way in which they themselves related to Jesus. Yet we have only established the basis for comparisons. We must still view the structures that arose on these foundations.

Each of our saints built a unique temple for the glory of God. Although all contain the essential architectural elements such as prayer life, the practice of virtue, and apostolic labor, we find points of difference. These flow directly from each one's special focus on the person of Jesus as revealed in the Gospels.

Before we proceed, it is absolutely necessary to be clear that the focus of the several spiritualities is just that — a focus. Each recognized, of course, the totality of the person of Jesus who is first of all and fundamentally the Son of God who became Man. To all of us He is indeed Friend and Master, Savior and Brother, Lord and Redeemer. Jesus is each of these, separately and together. Our saints responded to His call of love in accord with their natural attributes and insight, and by reason of the social and personal circumstances that surrounded their conversion. We know that through experience and prayer first attraction turns to spiritual familiarity, and the understanding of who Jesus is must necessarily deepen and broaden. If we do not embrace the entire person, the attraction settles into fantasy. Either the reality of love and commitment is accepted and becomes one's life, or the true Jesus will never be known. Yet the focus remains constant, as it does in every relationship.

This is how it was with each of our saints and is with any person seriously seeking to be holy, to live for God. Since a spirituality is a means toward union with God, it directs us toward specific religious goals, inspires us to particular devotional practices, and motivates us in the fulfillment of the duties of our state in life. If we do not follow faithfully in the way that we have been called by God's grace, difficulties from trials or persons will lead to confusion in our purpose. We will suffer what has been described as a "spiritual identity crisis" which will help neither ourselves nor the Church.

Also we might become very comfortable with the spirituality we ourselves follow. It works very well for us, and we could begin to feel that all others would be as well served if they came on the same journey. We might try to lead in our direction everyone over whom we have influence. That, of course, is the height of arrogance. The call to holiness comes from God, and the grace to reach such a goal is given by God. To help an individual discern the path on which he or she has been directed by grace is one thing; to urge them to follow the way that we travel reflects either pride or ignorance or both.

Books on the spiritual life that flow from an author's personal experience so often seem to have been written to guide everyone down the same road. If they contain much of spiritual substance, that is impossible. If they are written for beginners in the spiritual life, some general good will be accomplished. I believe, however, that spiritual books should target distinct groups, namely, those who follow one of the six basic spiritualities or any specification of them. When this is the case, they are very valuable. Even then each person's state of life should also be considered. For example, a book to guide married persons to sanctity should not be so vague as to cover all men and women who are married, but should reach to married persons who live by Franciscan spirituality, or Teresian, or Ignatian, or any of the others. They should be able to read about becoming saints through marriage, not just about living good and productive married lives.

Every priest who has worked extensively with parish communities, especially large ones, can understand what I mean. He has observed the great diversity of spiritual energies that exists among the most dedicated and saintly of God's people. Some rise naturally to roles of leadership without a trace of ambition. (We are not speaking here, obviously, of opportunists.) Others are content with and seek only to be one of those who help in the necessary preparation and clean-up work involved with the project at hand. Some function well only with the support of a group; others do better on their own with personalized tasks to perform on precise instructions. Some are interested in the promotion of prayer and devotional activities; others involve themselves in working with youth or the elderly. Some dedicate themselves to all kinds of work within the local church community; others are more into civic affairs. Some thrive in the public eye; others want to remain in the background. We cannot be content with an assumption that all these variations might be traced to differences in temperament. The pastor needs to identify which of his parishioners are truly motivated by the love of God, which ones are mired in false piety, and which ones are prompted more by natural propensities, however noble.

Looking at the varied *spiritual types* in a parish, we might be tempted to conclude that the intensely prayer-minded are akin to Saint Teresa, because their lives bespeak contemplation. Those who are attracted to group dynamics for the purpose of "getting things done" could be seen as faithful followers of Saint Ignatius. The more humble folk who are satisfied with being the helping hands would certainly remind us of Saint Francis. Those involved in the catechetical program, in spreading the truth of the Gospel, would be emulating Saint Dominic. Those fully taken up with planning and executing the parish's liturgical celebrations can be said to have the spirit of Saint Benedict. And those who organize efforts to influence the civic community with Gospel values could be seen as responding to the example of Saint Augustine.

All the above, of course, is somewhat simplistic. If we think about it, however, it is possible to recognize at least the kernel of truth. Some works do seem to be naturally reserved to the followers of particular spiritualities. Nevertheless, we do not claim that a particular type of work of itself excludes anyone (certainly not lay people), but we can expect that whatever work is performed will be motivated by a certain spirit. We know, for example, that all the *Great Six* were leaders. They were certainly not ambitious for personal glory, preferring to be simple disciples of Jesus. However, they understood that Jesus lived among us in obedience to His Father, and so they willingly accepted the call of God to lead. Yet we can easily recognize that the leadership style of each reflected a different spirit.

Up to now we have talked most directly about the six saints themselves, and they remain our inspiration in understanding the holiness of the Church and her devotional practices. The religious activities which they initiated or inspired have become an inseparable part of the fabric that constitutes our lives as the People of God. Very many currents of spiritual thought have entered the life of the Church from the principles of spirituality which they espoused. This is readily seen in the work and writings of the many saints who founded or reformed religious orders and congregations in subsequent centuries. Now is the time for us, therefore, to examine more closely the influence of our saints beyond the religious orders which carry on their traditions within the Church.

These orders and congregations are usually distinguishable from one another by such external factors as different community lifestyles which reflect their purpose and by distinguishable religious habits which identify their origins. They have distinct customs which promote the spirit in which they are formed, and their very apostolic preferences point up the

reason for their founding. Not all these, of course, are so evident that the members are always recognizable by a casual
observation. Within the same institute these externals vary
according to culture and are often different now than in past
eras. However, if we strip away the particular external characteristics of the separate forms of each religious tradition, influenced in whatever way by times and places, the authentic
spirit of each should be the same in Africa as in the United
States, or any other place, and likewise should be the same in
this generation as it was in the century of its origin. If the spirit
of any religious order cannot be identified so as to be distinct
from all the others, it has lost its credibility. If the difference
remains just external, the spirituality could be considered a
fraud.

What is required to express effectively an internal spirit
becomes more difficult to ascertain when we are speaking of
persons who are not religious, but who in their secular state
of life are pursuing holiness according to a particular spirituality tradition. The authentic spirit of each tradition does call
for some external expression, in which the circumstances of
time and place will play a part. To be legitimate, however, the
practices and style must be consistent with the principles of
the chosen spirituality.

Some Areas of Common Heritage

Before we concentrate on the essence of each spirituality in
more substantial ways, I would like to point to a few of the
more common devotional practices that have become inseparable from "being Catholic," and which are connected to the
different traditions. They are so part of our life today that their
origin and identity may not be universally appreciated. What
may have first flowed from a unique spirituality are now in
general use.

We properly consider in the first place devotions which

draw us close to Jesus Himself. A notable influence is attributed to Francis of Assisi, whose focus was on the human nature of Christ, especially on His simple lifestyle and the sufferings He endured to bring us salvation. He was the first (at Greccio in 1223) to gave us the representation of the birth of Jesus as a reminder of the humble circumstances in which the King of Kings was born. Setting up a crèche is now a universal custom at Christmas time. Francis also joyfully embraced personal difficulties and persecutions, in addition to work responsibilities and physical sufferings, as a bond with Jesus who had endured the same human condition. He wanted nothing more than to have his life mirror that of the Son of God. Franciscan preachers, notably Saint Leonard of Port Maurice, promoted the practice of accompanying Jesus to Calvary by making the Stations of the Cross as a way to understand the love of Jesus and to strengthen us as true disciples who follow Jesus in the carrying of the cross. This devotion is now a universal practice throughout the Church, especially during the season of Lent.

It is no mere coincidence that from the time of Saint Francis Christian art in the West began to present Christ in the realistic aspects of His human condition. Iconographic art, influenced by the ancient Church of the East, in which Christ and Mary and the saints are represented in majestic form, even when depicting a Gospel incident, was the prominent style everywhere until the thirteenth century.

Saint Teresa, like Saint Francis, focused our attention on the Sacred Humanity of Christ, but with a difference. Francis was content to reflect the life of Jesus as revealed in the Gospels. Teresa felt called to share in the very redemptive act itself because she experienced His love so strongly, and she needed to respond by uniting with Him in total surrender. She not only gladly offered her own sufferings and difficulties with those of Jesus, but undertook voluntary forms of penance. The recitation of the Morning Offering flows from this spirit as does the practice of offering up our tribulations for the salvation of souls. This tradition of self-abnegation also gave great impetus to the practice of private adoration before the Blessed Sacrament in order to strengthen awareness of the constant presence of Jesus who never ceases to love us.

This intimacy of love with Jesus that Teresa speaks about took special form in seventeenth century France in the preaching of St. John Eudes. He called the people to draw close to the heart of Jesus in prayer. This devotion was based on the emphasis by Saint Augustine that the love of Jesus, the Son of God made Man, draws us into the love of the Triune God, which is our ultimate goal. Devotion to the Sacred Heart of Jesus became a part of Catholic life throughout the world after Jesus revealed His love for us with the image of a flaming heart in an appearance to St. Margaret Mary Alacoque in 1674. Nor was devotion to the Heart of Mary far behind. Access to Jesus has always included a role for His mother. Since Augustine's admirable exposition of the place of Mary in relation to the Trinity, we have been reminded that Mary, the mother of the Son, is also the daughter of the Father and the spouse of the Holy Spirit.

Because she was an intimate partner of her Son in His mission of redemption for mankind, we need always to incorporate love for the Blessed Virgin Mary in our desire to know God. She is recognized as the one closest to Jesus, our model of faith and service. Since the Council of Ephesus in 431 this connection has been defended by the Church, and was strongly reinforced at the Second Vatican Council in 1964. In chapter eight of *Lumen Gentium* we read: *Mary... unites in her person and re-echoes the most important doctrines of the faith; and... she prompts the faithful to come to her Son, to his sacrifice and to the love of the Father.*

The *Great Six* have all given ample testimony about their love and affection for Mary as mother of Jesus, as mother of us all, and as mother of the Church. Each one added his/her own special emphasis. However, as Augustine himself had laid the theological foundation for any cult of Mary as fundamentally related to the mystery of the Trinity, his followers have fostered Marian devotion under specific titles: beginning with Our Lady of Perpetual Help, Our Lady of Good Counsel, and Mother of Consolation. Following in that tradition she has been given honor under many titles through the centuries, from those which extol her privileges (e.g., Our Lady of the Immaculate Conception) to those which emphasize her motherhood (e.g., Mother of Sorrows). As a loving mother, she is in every place and under all of life's circumstances where her children need her.

The devotion that has arisen in the Church as the foremost non-liturgical expression by which we give honor to Mary and seek her intercession is the recitation of the Rosary. It has reached such a place primarily by the efforts of the followers of Saint Dominic. Inspired by the great devotion to the Mother of God practiced by their founder, who himself came from the Augustinian tradition, Dominicans have from the time of Alan de la Roche at the end of the fifteenth century promoted the Confraternity of the Holy Rosary among the faithful.

What makes this Marian devotion so eminently Dominican is the content of the fifteen mysteries on which we meditate while praying the Hail Marys. We are contemplating the truths of our redemption together with the Mother of Jesus who was so intimately associated with them. We travel with her from the joyful moments of the Incarnation, through the sorrowful hours of His passion, to the glorious days of the Resurrection, and to her own place with the infant Church and in eternity. We unite in prayer both the intellect and the will, and arise strengthened in our commitment to make Jesus known by imitation of Mary in our daily life. The Rosary has kept us from the danger of the two extremes of Marian devotions, which make Mary more than the human being she is, however exalted, or which reduce her devotion to mere sentimentality. This contribution of the Dominican tradition, namely, the use of the Rosary with the accompanying meditations, has kept the balance between simple piety and the veneration of Mary in her unique place within the divine plan of salvation.

From the beginning, following the example of Jesus Himself, everyone who is serious about holiness of life has tried to "go away and rest awhile." They know the need to keep sight of our ultimate destination in the journey through this world. It is so easy to be distracted by pleasures and pains, to become side-tracked, and to be so absorbed by daily anxieties that we lose sight of life's purpose. The monastic tradition has always emphasized that we are all called to "live for God," and the monks of Saint Benedict from the beginning have offered any "busy" Christian the opportunity to "be alone with God." The monastic practice of *lectio divina* (spiritual reading, especially scriptural) was adopted by anyone who sought God in prayer, and is now a very wide-spread practice among serious Christians.

Since Benedictine monasteries are not accessible to everyone (nor are all interested in becoming a monk or nun even for a few days), the need has been satisfied in more recent times by many communities of religious who have established retreat houses, where laity (and religious) can enjoy this divine solitude. This movement has been especially influenced by the example of Saint Ignatius at Manresa and the subsequent practice of his followers to undergo a long period of retreat in preparation for their new life. Such a time away has had the effect of being more than a "spiritual rest," but a time of true conversion, a turning away from a former manner of living and toward a new commitment to Christ and His Church. This tradition is carried on today in new forms of retreat which are termed encounters.

We see that the spiritualities of the *Great Six* have permeated the devotional life of the entire Church. Since they do share so much in common (having the same source of grace and the same goal), it is not always easy to differentiate between their distinct pathways to holiness. But we must do this if their heritage is to be effective in our ecclesial life today. Three areas still call for review, namely, their contribution to a prayer tradition, their apostolic profile, and their motivation in the practice of the fundamental virtues.

CHAPTER SIX

THE PULSE OF AN INTERIOR LIFE

The most personal aspect of the spiritual life is the manner in which we pray, especially in the privacy of the heart. In this regard we need now to ask some fundamental questions about the various traditions of prayer that have come into the Church from the *Great Six*. Is there something distinct about Augustinian prayer that gives it a flavor which separates it from Franciscan prayer, and Franciscan prayer from any of the others? Are Benedictines so different from Jesuits when they pray? Has Dominic given us a style that distinguishes him from Teresa? When I reflect on the different paths each traveled on the way to holiness and their unique relationships with Jesus, I must answer affirmatively. They prayed in ways that were special to themselves. Although all had the same ultimate goal, namely union with the Triune God, and their separate ways eventually merged in the contemplative state, the points of origin were quite diverse. Their individual circumstances and personalities prompted different responses to the divine call. When they prayed, they were all unique children of the Heavenly Father.

Nor does the intimacy of personal prayer isolate us from others who are also friends of God. There is a link eventually to the prayer of the Church, that would especially include the Sacrifice of the Mass, but also recitation of the Canonical Hours that is prescribed by tradition for clergy and religious and participation in the popular devotions of the Christian community. Private and public forms of prayer are distinct, but they do relate to each other since the object of our affection is the same Person(s). Our saints brought their uniqueness also to public prayer.

This is readily understandable when we consider our relationship with a family member or friend, with whom we often speak privately, but sometimes join in a family dinner, on a work project, or in a recreational activity. We accept them in the context of their other relationships and their many interests which do not necessarily include us. The most powerful influence, however, in strengthening the bond of friendship always remains the quality conversation and time-sharing between two people. In like manner, our communication with the Father, through the Son, by the power of the Holy Spirit, may take various forms. We do not touch God directly by our own willing it, but are lifted up only after we have first reached out in prayer, which is done either in our private moments or in company with the Church.

Human beings are complex, formed by body and soul, mind and emotions. Parents who have raised more than one child know that each was a unique individual and has remained so throughout life. Their personality, experiences, and dreams had to be considered when speaking with them. In like manner, the *Great Six* each had a different approach to prayer, because it would flow from and into their unique spiritual instincts. This follows the spiritual maxim that grace builds on nature. We should expect that adherents of a particular tradition would want to follow the approach of the saint whose way directs their Christian life.

We can describe prayer simply as a "loving conversation with God." It is, therefore, not one-sided nor a shouting match nor a bargaining session. Because prayer is a conversation there must be a fair degree of listening, and this becomes the most difficult part. It is the part, however, that opens the soul to the thrust of grace. We are drawn into the life of the Triune God, through our personal bond with Jesus, the Son made

Man. This is called contemplation, i.e., to know the embrace of divine love.

Thus the more often we return to the solitude within ourselves, the greater force of love we experience. This will imbue us with greater zeal for God's glory and affect our subsequent return to daily work, responsibilities and apostolic efforts. Hence, in this regard, we have two aspects of our saints' approach to prayer that need to be looked at. First, we will examine the thrust of their prayer, i.e., how they expressed themselves in accord with the relationship they felt with Jesus. Secondly, we will consider how they prepared themselves to understand God's response in view of that personal connection.

We need to keep in mind what has already been said about the unique focus each saint had in his/her relationship to Jesus. All prayer must center on Jesus since we are joined to one God through the Second Person made Man who reveals the Father to us and from whom we receive the Holy Spirit. Our manner of prayer will not be identical with that of all good Christians, yet we will have much in common with others who see Jesus in the same way that we do. Our bond with Jesus will mirror that of one of the *Great Six*. Much will depend on personality, on experience, and on attitude toward ourselves as sinners. Let us find out to which of our saints we most relate.

How Apostles Pray

Augustine of Hippo gives us the perspective of one who lives with a strong awareness that each of us is in a continuing state of conversion, seeking out that for which we have been made, namely, union with the Triune God. His wonder at the marvelous destiny to which we have been called kept him turned toward God. He knew first-hand, however, the life-long struggle to put God first in every work and in every movement of the heart. We are held back from the full life of the Divine Persons by our own sensuality, our avarice, and our lust for power. He shows us that this struggle will not be won if we try to go on our own, but we must link ourselves with others among God's children for spiritual support. Those who have abandoned the call, or ignored it, will always try to draw us away into their own desolation.

Augustine was a busy man, especially in the affairs of the Church both within the Christian community and beyond, i.e. in her relationship to the wider civic community. He connected the concerns of those persons who needed his attention to the plan of God for all human beings. From his ever deepening faith in the mystery of God's life within us, nourished by extended periods of contemplative prayer, he sought to know what must be done for the greater good of God's people. He looked to see God's image in every person and to be sure that all men and women received the respect due them. Yet he remained conscious of the subtlety of pride. Hence, he looked for the signs of God's will not just from within himself but from the way others related to him, especially those involved in his daily life.

Those Christians who find themselves drawn to the wonder of God's love, but are often tempted to follow the way of those whose lives focus on this world's pleasure and glory, need to learn the valuable lesson from Augustine that in our prayer we must use the Scriptures, especially the Gospels, epistles of Saint Paul, and the psalms. He showed us that prayer must express the wonder that the Scriptures reveal. Our lifestyle, too, must reflect an ordered discipline over our physical and intellectual powers that will minimize the pull of sinful nature, and open us up to marvel at and revel in the wonderful state to which we have been called as children of God. The *Rule* of Saint Augustine, although written specifically for religious, can be a guide for everyone. The principles which it espouses are fundamental to growth in the spiritual life, in the search for holiness.

To be conscious of our fundamental relationship to the Triune God, through the Son made Man, is what we learn from Augustine. Because he was caught up in work which put him in the forefront of the Church's life, he could not afford to be distracted from the proper balance between affairs of the spirit and the affairs of this world. His example of prayer is not just for bishops, however, but for civil officials, executives of large businesses, social workers, etc. — whoever must confront the evil of the world head on. Those who are placed in positions of responsibility, who are called to find solutions to the problems of an ever-changing society without compromising the Truth, find in Augustine the guide to prayer that will keep them always reminded that each and every person has been made in the image of God, with whom we share a common destiny, namely, union with God through the Spirit who dwells in the Church, the Body of Christ.

> You are great, O Lord, and greatly to be praised: great is your power and your wisdom is without measure. And man, so small a part of your creation, wants to praise you: this man, though clothed with mortality and bearing the evidence of sin and the proof that you withstand the proud. Despite everything, man, though a small part of your creation, wants to praise you. You yourself encourage him to delight in your praise, for you have made us for yourself, and our heart is restless until it rests in you.
> *Confessions of Saint Augustine*

Augustine drew strength from the God-Man Jesus as a friend who showed him the power of love. Our saint looked inside his memory, fed by the Scriptures, to find the God of love. He urges us always to be aware of the dignity we share as children of God, so that we will not be drawn to compromise the divine mysteries. In our conversations with Jesus we will speak from a consciousness of the weakness of our resources and the pride of our fallible reasoning. Faith will open our understanding to God's ways and strengthen our loyalty to

Jesus and to the Church through which He passes on the Truth that leads us to salvation and eternal glory.

Augustine calls us to a life that embodies a routine of physical and intellectual discipline as a foundation for prayer. Also he teaches us to be close to the Virgin Mary who shares the life of the Blessed Trinity more intimately than any of us since she was the mother of the Second Person made Man. We will find the resolve to give ourselves for the salvation of souls in the strength of the Eucharist, where the sacrifice of Jesus is offered to the Father by a people united to each other in the Holy Spirit. Through His Body and Blood we truly are one with the Blessed Trinity.

A synthesis of the Augustinian way of prayer and life can be found in the eighth chapter of the Saint Paul's Letter to the Romans. Those who would pray as Augustine did should read this chapter often as a point of reflection. Together with a designated time of prayer each day and participation in the celebration of the Eucharist, we have the foundation needed to grow in the holiness exemplified by the life of Augustine. All else that fills out the Christian life finds a beginning here.

Yet there are some who have another approach. They are called to fulfill the responsibility of passing on the faith, by word or example, to individuals or specific groups. The most evident examples of such persons are parents and catechists who find that they must look to Jesus as the Divine Wisdom who came to live among us. They relate to Him as the Teacher who has shown us how to prepare others to receive the truth. He reached them not only with formal teachings but with the compassion of kind words and deeds. He offered all His energies and His very life for their salvation. To speak with Jesus as the divine teacher and as the eternal priest who offered His life for His people is the essence of Dominican prayer.

Dominic, as a Canon Regular, came from the Augustinian tradition but was drawn into circumstances that called for something more expansive, to go in person to far places where the Lord's truth was needed. The patrimony of the Church had been ravaged by the failure to teach the Truth in the Person of Jesus crucified, and to keep the Church herself from the influence of a civic society torn by fraternal strife. Large numbers of people were being lost to heresy because of ignorance concerning the real Jesus and the true nature of the Church as the sacrament of salvation. Too often this happened because the *students* did not see in the *teacher* the example given us by Jesus. Dominican prayer seeks to identify with Jesus as the Truth who has come down from heaven and who shows us by example the way to eternal life.

Dominic formed his life to the image of Jesus crucified, and spent much time in contemplation before the cross of his Savior. He went forth to preach by word and example what he had learned from Jesus in prayer, that our lives must be spent to bring to Jesus the souls He has redeemed by His blood. In addition to the study of Scripture, the indispensable preparation to fulfill the responsibility of teaching divine truth is to be one with the Church in prayer, especially at the Sacrifice of the Mass. To be truly the presence of Christ in the world calls for the practice of mortification that channels our pride and sensuality toward a life which mirrors that of Jesus, through whom we have been made into the image of God. Dominic prayed to Jesus as his Savior, and joined with Him as priest, who had offered Himself for the salvation of souls through suffering, good works, and preaching.

May God the Father bless us,
May God the Son heal us,
May God the Holy Spirit enlighten us and give us eyes to see with,
　　　ears to hear with,
　　　and hands to do the work of God with,
　　　feet to walk with,
　　　and a mouth to preach the word of salvation with,
　　　and the angel of peace to watch over us and lead us at last,
　　　by our Lord's gift, to the kingdom. Amen.

A Dominican Blessing

An indispensable aspect of Dominican prayer is the attention given to the Blessed Virgin Mary as the one who can best lead us to the knowledge of Jesus and help us understand the love that brought Him to the cross. Dominic spoke to Mary as the mother who offered up her son for the salvation of those to whom we are called to teach the Truth. All are her children. Dominic taught us to seek through her the graces needed so that our mouths will always speak blessings and our hands will always bring comfort to those we meet.

Thus we find the spirit of gratitude for God's goodness (the prayer of *wonder*) as the highlight of Augustine's prayer, and the sense of moral and intellectual need (prayer of *entreaty*) to be reflective of Dominic's converse with God. Others among our fellow Christians, however, feel a frustration that calls for a different approach. They find themselves busy about so many things that they are conscious of the deficiencies in their daily efforts to be faithful to Jesus. They find that a spirit of urgency about the work that needs to be done can turn into an activism which reflects oneself rather than the Person of the Son of God. They do not just want to *work* for Him but rather always to remember that they are serving their Lord at every moment in the fulfillment of the mission He began on earth. Such persons find in Ignatius of Loyola the guide to a prayer relationship with Jesus that calls for a determined preparation, and a daily accounting of our efforts to fulfill the Christian calling.

Perhaps because he had been a soldier, Ignatius developed a prayer style that might be called realistic. He had come to recognize that the human need to have a sense of accomplishment often leads to personal vanity. True devotion to the Lord demands loyalty to His cause, a goal that is undermined by selfishness and moral cowardice. Hence, he began with an evaluation of his strengths and weaknesses, where and how he showed a propensity to sin. This approach takes up the first week of his *Spiritual Exercises.* Then only does he focus his meditations on the life, passion and resurrection of Christ, and this continues to constitute the power of Ignatian prayer, bringing about the growth and strength of one's love for the Lord Jesus.

Those who have a strong desire to love and serve the Lord but are overwhelmed by great distractions in the manifold aspects of their busy lives may find that they have an affinity to Ignatius. To be drawn by Jesus into the circle of His companions in order to help carry out the work He began requires faithfulness to Him and to the Church which He built on Peter. This spirit is cultivated by a prayer life that constantly seeks to know the Lord's mind from the Scriptures, and be strengthened by His presence in the Eucharist in offering the Sacrifice of the Mass.

Ignatian prayer is centered in meditation on the actions and words of Jesus and in contemplation of their significance to our daily life with Him. The Gospels reveal the mystery of the Son of God made Man in the concrete situations of His life, from birth, throughout His public life, and in the events surrounding His passion and resurrection. The ample use of the imagination during meditation will relate scriptural events to the current situation we face, the experience of carrying the Gospel message of redemption into daily life. It matters little whether our work is directly Church-related or concerns itself with the many tasks by which we fulfill our daily social and family responsibilities.

Thus Ignatius teaches us to "find God in all things" so that we become familiar with the way God acts and recognize that He is always present to us. In this way we become "contemplative in action." Hence, the manner in which we undertake our work must show the presence of God's love in the world. As companions of Jesus, the Lord of all, the goal is to know Him more intimately and "keep on the move" toward becoming a more effective instrument of His glory, in both sacred and mundane endeavors.

> Take, Lord, and receive all my liberty, my memory, my understanding, and my entire will — all that I have and call my own. You have given it all to me. To you, Lord, I return it. Everything is yours; do with it what you will. Give me only your love and your grace. That is enough for me.
> *Spiritual Exercises*, Fourth Week

All of us make choices daily that either give greater glory to God or further only our own interests. Even when our lives are centered on the work of Jesus, in deeds of charity, in teaching others the mysteries of salvation, or in running programs that build up the kingdom of God, we feel called to do a better job today than we did yesterday. Ignatius teaches us that we accomplish this by relating our personal daily experiences in His service to appropriate accounts in the Gospel.

Such an examen makes us increasingly aware of how God has been present to us in the actions of the day, or indeed how we might have forgotten Him. This is the heart of what might be called the Ignatian prayer of *faithfulness*, because it shows up areas that reveal a lack of generosity in our efforts. As did John the beloved disciple, we stay close to Jesus at the foot of the cross (loyal always in the face of adversity), and then look to Mary our Mother as the Mother of the Church, and find in her love every reason to offer ourselves for the salvation of souls.

We can see that the distinct ways of prayer which the Church has received from Augustine, Dominic and Ignatius are geared toward the fulfillment of a commitment to the proclamation of the Gospel. Although their prayers express different relationships to Jesus as Friend, as Savior, or as Lord, each saint is asking for understanding and support in order to fulfill the work assigned him. What they seek is an intimate bond with Jesus. Although the calling of each of these saints as priest flowed into their prayers, their styles are possible to whomever is called as an apostle and sent forth to proclaim the Good News of salvation, whether such apostles are religious or laity, married or single. From unique perspectives Augustinian, Dominican and Ignatian prayer styles are properly termed apostolic.

To Know Him Is to Love Him

We now turn our attention to the other three saints whose prayer life was based more on their desire to know the person of Jesus Himself rather than on the work they felt called to do for Him. Benedict, Francis and Teresa sought a close union with God, and their search brought them to a love for all those whom God had created and redeemed. This called for sharing the love of God with others. In so doing they became an example to them of God's presence, a support in need, and an encouragement in the practice of virtue. Benedict and his monks, in their solitude, joined prayer and the ordinary work of the day as they sought to become worthy sons of God. Francis and his friars praised God in prayer for the same reason that they imitated the lifestyle of Jesus, to give glory to His Father. Teresa and her nuns, as daughters of Mary, abandoned themselves to God's will in lives of prayer that they might join Jesus in His redemptive mission.

Benedictine prayer seeks a union with God that is most direct. It nurtures a spirit of solitude in the midst of a routine day that pulses between prayer of *adoration* and the hours of labor required to support the exigencies of our physical and intellectual life. It recognizes that our unity with God grows with and through those persons with whom we share our lives as we fulfill the responsibilities that we have assumed. As disciples of Jesus, those who pray with Benedict do not let the demands on their time and energies deny them the right to be close to Him, who alone can show us the Father and share with us the Holy Spirit. Secure in one place, they find the hidden life of Jesus to be a comfort and model.

Most Christians who pray the Benedictine way are not

monks or nuns, but they are persons who for the most part find themselves occupying a limited world, which may nevertheless be extremely full. They have days which are filled with the ordinary affairs of living and do not want to lose the essential purpose of the Christian calling — to seek God. To do this there is need to organize the day so that there is a rhythm of work and prayer (*ora et labora*). The *Rule* of Saint Benedict is full of practical norms for making the most of each day's work and each encounter with others who share our life. He applies them to the family of monks and their relationship to each other and the outside world. Nevertheless, the principles are equally applicable to anyone who as part of any "family" grouping seeks to make its life secure and productive with spiritual and temporal blessings.

The Benedictine way has its foundation in the life of the Church assembled at prayer. To keep that balance of work and prayer focused on God, a determined effort is made to participate in the Church's full liturgical life in addition to private prayer and attendance at Mass. For some this might include the daily recitation of the Canonical Hours.

> And first of all, whatever good work you begin to do, beg of Him with most earnest prayer to perfect it, that He who has now deigned to count us among His sons may not at any time be grieved by our evil deeds. For we must always so serve Him with the good things He has given us, that He will never as an angry Father disinherit His children, nor ever as a dread Lord, provoked by our evil actions, deliver us to everlasting punishment as wicked servants who would not follow Him to glory. Prologue, *Rule of Saint Benedict*

When we use the method of private prayer that monks have bequeathed to us, we make the effort to spend some quiet time alone each day, however brief. The regular and conscious contact with God the Father through meditation on the life of the Son of God made Man gives us an openness to the inspirations of the Holy Spirit. This process, which leads toward the contemplation of the divine mysteries, is called *Lectio Divina* (Sacred Reading). Our prayer may begin with a reading from the Scriptures (emphasizing the psalms, the Gospels, and the Pauline epistles), slowly and with sufficient pause for meditation on the meaning of the text. But any book of a spiritual nature may be used. We then apply to our work and to the people whom we will encounter during that day whatever insights that we receive, and come to an understanding of what God expects of us. His divine will is revealed and the grace of the Holy Spirit compels us to act accordingly. And we must continually look to Mary, the mother of Jesus, who was the first to whom the mystery of salvation was revealed and who can assist us to ponder the Word of God in our hearts.

In contrast to the orderly style of the Benedictines, the followers of Saint Francis seem to follow no rules when they pray. The Little Poor Man of Assisi spent his time in the praise of God for whatever he was experiencing at the moment. He knew that God is good and all His works are praiseworthy. Since he began with what was at hand and moved about from place to place, he praised God for that day, that person, that pain, that gift, that sorrow, that joy. It is no wonder that Franciscans are said to pray with their eyes open.

Francis himself so enjoyed *being alone with God* in contemplative prayer that he often spent long periods in the mountains away from the bustle of human affairs. He was often reluctant to return, and one time wondered whether God even wanted him to resume life among the people. This temptation was dispelled with the help of Saint Clare and a holy friar named Masseo. With the divine will for him confirmed, he resumed his journey through the world of men, continuing to praise God for the sun in the heavens and the birds in the sky, for every individual he met, regardless of social status, and indeed for all His creatures. Above all things, Francis praised the Father for sending Jesus to live among us as our brother.

Francis passionately desired to know Jesus, about how He

lived on earth as contained in the Gospels, and about His dealings with the people He encountered. The imitation of the earthly life of Jesus was the goal Francis saw as the perfect expression of love. He wanted to be powerless as the omnipotent Son of God who allowed Himself to be crucified, to be poor as the King of the Universe who was born in the poverty of a stable, to be humble as the Master who washed the feet of His disciples. Francis prayed for the privilege to share that life, even to the pain of being nailed to the cross. He lived that final request for his last two years when he bore the stigmata, the five wounds of Jesus, as he had asked. Francis wanted to share in particular the life of those whom Jesus favored, i.e., the poor, the sick, and the outcasts of society. He lived himself as one of the poor and among the lepers. His prayer emanated from this perspective, and in spite of his romantic reputation Francis was very human and down-to-earth.

Those who pray with Francis are those who identify with the very human Christ, who know the struggles, sorrows and disappointments of life and readily see in them the will of the Father who did not spare His own Son these same tribulations. They live the beatitudes as the essence of the Gospel, and seek to be in particular instruments of peace among brothers and sisters who do not see poverty, sickness, and hard work as blessings from God. They seek to show joy when life's circumstances make it difficult to be thankful for God's goodness. Their strength comes from knowing that each day is a share in the Son of God's own life here on earth. They do not simply want to follow Jesus as disciples and carry their own cross behind Him, but to embrace Jesus as He hangs upon the cross. Their union with Jesus in prayer is simple, no special formulas, like lovers being content in each other's company or like brothers sharing the same experience. Franciscan prayer is one of *praise* for the all-holy God. The Sacrifice of the Mass and the presence of Jesus in the Blessed Sacrament is a constant reminder of the goodness of the Father who sent His Son to live among us.

Most high, all-powerful, all good, Lord!
  All praise is yours, all glory, all honor and all blessing.

All praise be yours, my Lord, through all that you have made,
  And first my Lord Brother Sun,
  Who brings the day; and light you give to us through him.

All praise be yours, my Lord, through Sister Water,
  So useful, lowly, precious and pure.

All praise be yours, my Lord, through those who grant pardon
  For love of you; through those who endure sickness
  and trial.

Praise and bless my Lord, and give him thanks.
                    — from St. Francis' *Canticle of Brother Son*

Francis had a great love for Mary, the mother of Jesus, and honored her as the one who shared His life most intimately from Bethlehem and Nazareth to the foot of the cross and after the resurrection. He was grateful that she made Jesus our brother and offered Him for our salvation. Francis understood that she, as His mother, is able to bring us near to her son and help us appreciate, if not understand, the love which brought Him to the cross.

Up to now we have shown that five of our saints had their special approaches to prayer which reflect different relationships toward Jesus in their commitment to His kingdom. We can appreciate how each of them contributed to the holiness of the Church. Even the images we have in our mind's eye of Augustine, Benedict, Dominic, Francis, and Ignatius reveal very distinct personalities, and indicate why their disparate styles address the varied circumstances under which Christians live.

In speaking of the prayer life of each one, we have avoided the word "mystic," although all of them in their own way were mystics. In due time, their souls reached the heights of intimacy with God. However, it is not easy to categorize the prayer style of the last of our saints since the word "mystic" is always associated with her name. In fact, Teresa of Avila's manner of prayer appears to encompass the styles of all the others. Her writings, in which she draws on her own mystical experiences, are so extensive and profound that Pope Paul VI declared her a Doctor of the Church.

But on examination (here I bow to those scholars who have studied her writings extensively, as I do to those who have written about our other saints), I have concluded that this very inclusiveness gives her the uniqueness that is Carmelite. Hers is the white light that results from the union of the varied hues of the rainbow. Let us review the perspectives on Jesus of our saints. The Second Person as man draws us into the life of the Trinity (Augustinian prayer of *wonder*). Jesus, Son of God, calls us to give glory to the Father as His adopted children (Benedictine prayer of *adoration*). Jesus asks us to help Him fulfill his mission of salvation through the Church which He established (Dominican prayer of *entreaty*). Jesus having come among us as our brother is a reason to be grateful at every moment for God's goodness (Franciscan prayer of *praise*). We have a constant need to be vigilant in light of our weakness so that as companions of Jesus we will faithfully promote the glory of God and His kingdom (Ignatian prayer of *faithfulness*).

There seems to be nothing left, except to look upon one's entire life as a prayer. That is the gift of Saint Teresa to the Church, to teach us how one goes about it. This she has done by reviewing her own experiences at prayer in her *Autobiography*. In *The Way of Perfection* she outlines what is needed to attain holiness, especially mortification of one's senses and detachment from worldly ambitions. She leads us through six antechambers into the inner mansions of the *Interior Castle*, which is the state of passive contemplation. It could be said from an overall evaluation that in some way she covers the particular emphases of the other five.

Yet she too is unique, for she has a different focus on the person of Jesus. Her gaze is on the cross of the Redeemer, and her ear attuned to His cry: *My God, my God, why have you forsaken me?* (Ps 22:1). She calls us to give ourselves in total abandonment to the will of God in all circumstances, so that our love may be purified. As mother of the Redeemer, Mary is her model, taking as her prayer of surrender the words of the Blessed Virgin at the Annunciation: *Behold, I am the handmaid of the Lord. May it be done to me according to your word* (Lk 1:38).

Teresa *offered* up all her work, trials, and physical pain for the success of the Church's mission to bring salvation to sinners. She dedicated her life as a sacrifice in union with the cross of Jesus for the redemption of the world. All her prayer to this end came together in the Mass as the memorial of the death of the Redeemer, and in the Eucharist she found that closeness to Jesus which is indispensable for anyone who wants to share His suffering.

Let nothing disturb you,	All things come together
Let nothing affright you,	For those who possess God.
For all things are passing;	Nothing is lacking,
Only God is unchanging.	Since God alone suffices.
Be patient.	*Bookmark of Saint Teresa*

We can readily see who would immediately find in Teresa's prayer of *surrender* the way to a close bond with Jesus. Would it not be anyone who finds that the suffering, disappointments, injustices, boredom, and other difficulties that life inflicts on us are insupportable without the value that is given them by the death of Jesus? *Now I rejoice in my sufferings for your sake, and in my flesh I am filling up what is lacking in the afflictions of Christ on behalf of His body, which is the Church* (Col 1:24). This would especially be those who are afflicted with chronic illnesses, suffer from unjust social conditions, are trapped in oppressive working situations, etc. But are not the everyday burdens of life enough? To be sure. So Teresian prayer is available to all Christians who look forward to those quiet moments in every day when they can pour out their hearts to God, gather up their efforts to live His will, and place them on the altar of sacrifice as an offering for their own sins as well as for the salvation of all sinners.

* * * *

We have contrasted the prayer style of the *Great Six*. We note only what is essential to mark the differences among them and which directs them toward the goal of holiness, union with the Triune God. For an in-depth study of any of them, a good spiritual library is full of books to choose from.

Holiness does not begin and end with prayer, although the bond of love between God and each of us will wither without a prayer life. However, that bond is fed and nourished also by the appropriate response of the lover to the needs of the beloved. As lovers of God in this world we have been sent by Jesus, as members of His Body, the Church, to do our part in the fulfillment of His mission in this world. Not everyone has been sent to do everything, although each of us has an indispensable role. It behooves us now to examine the specific responsibilities of those who have been called to follow the way of holiness of each of our saints.

CHAPTER SEVEN

SENT BY JESUS INTO EVERY PLACE

This book adds to the cascade of writings on the spiritual life that have deluged the Church in the past thirty years. That fact, plus the abundance of committees, programs and encounter groups that have arisen for the strengthening of the bond of charity among the People of God, would make one think that the zeal of Christians is poised to conquer the effects of sin and to unite all to Christ. A quick look around will assure us that it has not happened and likely never will, certainly not in any two successive generations. But we can be thankful that there is a new sense of mission in our time among those seriously committed to Jesus and the Gospel. Since the close of the Second Vatican Council, more laymen realize that the world is not saved, nor do we attain holiness, unless we take on the apostolic mission of Jesus. That calls for all the baptized to spread the Good News, wherever and however we have been graced to do so.

There is certainly no lack of activity in this regard, even with the dwindling number of priests and religious. The laity in many quarters have taken up the challenge, and have responded with holy zeal. We might review the complaint that the laity have begun to act like clergy, and the clergy are taking on the social responsibilities of laymen. However, whatever truth that allegation has, I believe it is only a temporary point of confusion until the post-Vatican II generation sorts out the needs and limitations in each area of the apostolic life.

One reason for the current difficulty might well be that the prayer life and the apostolic commitment of many are operating on two separate planes. This cannot be intentional, but it does illustrate a crisis of spiritual identity. Let us now concentrate on the challenge of the apostolic dimension of holiness. We want to be faithful to the mission which we each have from God, lest we be liable to the judgment: *I did not send these prophets, yet they ran. I did not speak to them, yet they prophesied* (Jr 23:21).

We need to keep in mind the apostolic commitment that tradition has allotted to those who follow the particular ways of the *Great Six.* In their respective generations they had an impact in a special area of Church life. These apostolic purposes are embodied in the religious families which still look to these saints for example and inspiration. We might have need to question the extent they may have modified or strayed from the particular work that was assigned to them for the building up the Body of Christ. As we look for their response to the Church's efforts at renewal today, we should expect to see in each a different apostolic profile comparable to the need that was fulfilled when the tradition began.

We can wonder whether this lack of apostolic focus might be contributing to the numerical decline within religious orders and congregations today. The greater concern is that this confusion limits the effectiveness of the countless lay men and lay women who are taking on the responsibility of the apostolic mission of the Church. They look to religious for guidance in their spiritual lives but often find the directions confusing.

The Church in our day has formerly declared that she is in need of a renewal. This call was issued in 1965 through the sixteen documents of the Second Vatican Council. With the wisdom of great experience she first re-affirms through the four documents called Constitutions the essential truths and principles that cannot be compromised. These concern her nature (*Lumen Gentium*), her foundation in divine revelation (*Dei Verbum*), her experience as a worshipping community in the celebration of the Eucharist (*Sacrosanctum Concilium*), and her role as the instrument of salvation to the world (*Gaudium et Spes*). The search for a renewed spirit toward Gospel simplicity must not compromise the will of Christ. The documents imply, however, that we do need to replace the non-essentials which are hindering true evangelization in our changed society.

We are reminded of a lament made by Angelo Roncalli on the day of his coronation as Pope John XXIII in 1958, as he surveyed the panorama of pageantry that extended around him: "Indeed, this is a far cry from the Sea of Galilee." Like so many stories about John, this one too may be apocryphal. Yet we know that he did take almost immediate action toward reform, in some cases by a stroke of his pen, and finally in his call for an ecumenical council "to let in some fresh air" so the Church might move toward *aggiornamento*.

The Council affirmed in three Declarations the value of Christian education, the holy bond between Christians and Jews, and the freedom of conscience for all. Each of these has its own importance in a renewed Church. The specific call, however, for a comprehensive renewal is found in the nine Decrees which address the practical and temporal aspects of the Church's life. The Council Fathers recognized that something new was required in this generation if she were to be faithful.

The first Decree places the modern means of communication at the service of the Gospel and also challenges Catholics to enter the field of the secular mass media. The growing power of radio and television, film and theater, must be harnessed for the spread of the kingdom of light to counter the influence of the culture of darkness. In a second Decree we find confirmed the pre-eminence of the Catholic Eastern Churches in the development of liturgy and theology in

Christianity's beginning and their importance as an expression of the Church's universality. Through their strengthening the Church can better reach out to the alienated Orthodox brethren. A third Decree extends a fraternal embrace toward the non-Catholic Christian Churches of the West, in order to remove centuries of suspicion which has been an obstacle to the unity for which Christ prayed. Hence, we see that these first three Decrees essentially call for a change of attitude, which will serve as the foundation of reform in the structures and procedures that must open up the power of the Catholic Faith in every place, in every nation, and in every culture.

Real and substantial renewal is outlined in the other six Decrees and these affect the specific responsibilities of all Church members, namely, bishops and priests, religious and laity, within their own nations and beyond. No one yet claims that the reforms envisioned by these six documents have been fully realized. We might legitimately wonder whether we can place some responsibility for this with the followers of the spirituality traditions whose very purpose for being was to bring about a renewed vigor to the Body of Christ. A review of the areas which were addressed for renewal indicate that each tradition bears a direct relationship to the Council's goals. Has the opportunity been missed because the religious who embody these traditions are still searching for their own identity in this post-conciliar Church?

The 5th, 13th and 16th Centuries All Over Again

As in the time of Augustine and Benedict, the Church today has a problem with the dissemination among the faithful of false doctrines by her own, and also faces a society that is more interested in its own fulfillment than in the rights of God. Similarly, as in the time of Dominic and Francis, today's clergy find they have a lessening respect and influence among the body of the faithful. Then too, not unlike the time of Ignatius and Teresa, our Christian people today suffer from an alarming ignorance of their Faith. The influence of those in religious life is also declining, although at the same time we are witnessing a growing interest in the spiritual life among the Catholic laity. The Church sent out the alarm at the Second Vatican Council, and these very issues are addressed in the six Decrees from the Council which concern the place and function of bishops, priests, religious, and laity in the life of the Church.

The *Decree on the Pastoral Office of Bishops in the Church* has called for a closer collaboration of the successors of the apostles with each other and with the pope, in their joint responsibility for the universal Church. As the custodian of revealed truth in his diocese, the bishop is challenged to proclaim boldly the teachings of Christ and to promote an orthodox catechesis that reaches to all segments of the People of God. Together with his priests, the Ordinary is the sign of unity between his diocese and the universal Church, and with the pope, who as Vicar of Christ is her chief shepherd. The primary link is one of faith, in Jesus who is Lord, in His Church which is His Body, and in the Sacraments which sanctify the Church by the grace won through His death on the Cross.

This is nothing new. What is new is the call for a closer relationship of the bishops with each other in several new structures (e.g., bishops' conferences), and for the bishop to have a more fraternal and pastoral relationship with his priests, and a closer involvement in the lives of his people. The bishops who attended the Second Vatican Council recognized that they must lead the way, if true renewal were to take place. They had no choice but to assume the responsibility. Christ had put them in charge.

We might wonder how this condition of the Church's faltering influence had come about. The bishops seem to be admitting that the inaction of many bishops to safeguard the faith, often against attacks from within, and their hesitancy to lead their priests in the ways of the Spirit had allowed the need for renewal to reach a serious level. In some ways the bishops of the Council had looked for their inspiration from Augustine of Hippo, perhaps the greatest of their number since Saint Paul and who is quoted so frequently in the conciliar documents. He not only left to the Church a thorough exposition and defense of the fundamental truths of faith, which the pope and bishops pass on to succeeding generations. He also brought to his colleagues in the episcopacy of his day an example of how bishops were to live, if their words were to be believed by those of weak faith.

Yet we know that structural changes do not get to the source of the problems. The very fabric of the Church's unity is threatened today, as it is in each generation, by those who forget the truth that her life is founded on the mystery of the Triune God. Any determination of which structures to abandon and what new procedures to pursue must flow from a faith that is solidly based on revealed Truth. The Church's history so often shows that timidity in matter of renewal only postponed the inevitable, as was evident at the time of the Protestant Revolution. True reform begins when Peter walks on water. As in the past, notably the feudal days, the Church finds herself trapped in political and/or economic alliances, especially on local levels. She is confronted with the demands of human prudence and the wisdom of the social sciences. Today she needs the spirituality forces of the *Great Six* to be galvanized as they were in the 5th, 13th, and 16th centuries, in accord with their respective charisms, to bring the Church into a true reform that is dictated by faith. Each tradition must recognize its special responsibility in bringing the People of God to renewal.

Each Tradition Has a Specialty

I am going to suggest, audaciously, that the forces of each spirituality should concentrate on the goals that are elucidated in very specific documents and let the other traditions handle what they are best equipped to do. This will assist the Church to reach the reform level envisioned by the Fathers of the Second Vatican Council. The respective institute must find its niche in the multi-leveled thrust of Church renewal, and at the same time discover its own identity in our age. The traditions are paired as they were in history and joined with the documents to which they relate. Each brought renewal to the Church from complementary perspectives, one from the apostolic thrust ("what has to be done") and the other from the charismatic view (the "how" of Gospel style).

Schematically, let us take an over-all look at the Decrees with the spirituality traditions that I believe relate to them, and then I will follow with my reasons for each alignment.

Augustinian / Benedictine:	Catholic Eastern Churches
	Ecumenism
	Pastoral Office of Bishops in the Church
Dominican / Franciscan:	Up-to-date Renewal of Religious Life
	Training of Priests
	Ministry and Life of Priests
Ignatian / Teresian:	Means of Social Communication
	Apostolate of Lay People
	Church's Missionary Activity

This list does not imply absolute exclusiveness, e.g., that Franciscans should have nothing to do with ecumenism. Rather we wish simply to point out where the respective traditions have the most to offer, namely, those areas of renewal which best fit the apostolic profile of the various spiritualities.

To begin: Augustinian spirituality looks outward to the broad spectrum of human nature and sees each person as a child of God who reflects the life of the Trinity. The Benedictine approach is a reminder that we have been made for God, and that our life must transcend the mundane in which we are immersed by human necessity and the will of God. Both are shrouded in the aura of mystery that surrounds our relation to the divine. Their origins have root in the apostolic and monastic traditions of the Eastern Churches, from Anthony to Basil. So who better to develop rapport with the *Catholic Eastern Churches*, especially when they function in areas where the Church of the West predominates? Augustinian support for them on the apostolic level and Benedictine cooperation on the liturgical level would help alleviate the fear among the Orthodox East that to unite with Rome is to deny their ecclesiastical traditions. The followers of Augustine and Benedict are the natural link between East and West.

There is easily seen also a natural connection of Augustine and Benedict to the broader field of *Ecumenism* since dialogue with non-Catholic Christian Churches of the West is concerned with grace and freedom, faith and practice, sacraments and authority. The Protestant assertion that the Catholic Church has broken with the Apostolic traditions is easily put aside by the evidence of her connection to the patristic age, since Augustine's theology and Benedict's style of life are in place today. The accouterments of worship and ecclesial style may have changed (and these are legitimate objects of reform), but the dogmatic and sacramental link is unbroken. The Augustinian program offers direction toward a simplification of Church life, and the Benedictine way can tap into the spiritual energy that is evident within Protestant religious traditions.

We must recognize that there are legitimate complaints of non-Catholic Christians that we have complicated the Gospel, especially in matters of style (triumphalism) and authority (use of non-spiritual power). Some have suggested that our bishops must return in some manner to the simpler style of the early Church. In this regard we can do no better than be guided by Augustine and Benedict. This would include, of necessity, the reforms called for in the Decree concerning the *Pastoral Office of Bishops*, to which we have already alluded and which has the shadow of Saint Augustine hovering over it.

Nor must we lose sight of the Benedictine influence on the life of bishops in the early Middle Ages. Many monks were called to the episcopacy, as well as others who had been trained by monks, not the least of which was Pope Saint Gregory the Great. The observation has been made that the lifestyle of our bishops and their tendency to be insulated by ranks of clerical bureaucrats have weakened their moral authority, not only among the faithful but in secular society as well. Might not the community style of monastic life be the image to be imitated in the diocesan structure, with the bishop holding the place of Christ and functioning in the same way as the abbot with his community? These are only musings, but it might prove beneficial for our bishops to confer with the Benedictines, and look for guidance in the simplification of their lives. The monks also could use the insights to know their own place in the Church's life today.

We do not want to exclude the Catholic laity from this call to reform in any of our references to the conciliar documents. Those who follow the Augustinian way, for example, are generally the "movers" of society, the "bishops" of the secular city. Whether in the public arena or in business, they too, as committed Christians, must not use their position of advantage for their personal advancement, but are called to serve the common good of God's people. Also men and women who follow Benedict's way are the "monks" and "nuns" in secular society with their example of fidelity to God within daily circumstances. Their influence may extend only to a select circle of family, friends, or co-workers, but it will be deep and have a ripple effect in the broad society. By a faith-filled obedience to the divine will, they show forth a holy generosity in everyday life that reflects the presence of God among His people. These "bishops," "monks" and "nuns" will fulfill the mission of Christ among people and in places where the official ones never go.

Now let us move to a lower tier in the *hierarchy* of Church life, those areas which touch the lives of *ordinary* people in the place where all of us live, i.e., our parish community. We refer to the place of priests and religious in the life of the Church, and recall the influence which Dominic and Francis had on the renewal of the priesthood and religious life in their day. This perspective was so central to their way that both of them strongly opposed their friars becoming bishops. When one considers the authority it confers, it certainly does seem that the miter is inappropriate for one committed to being part of the minor class (Franciscans). Also Dominicans are expected to go everywhere that the truth must be preached, and do not need the responsibility of governing since their call is not limited to one place or community.

Dominic was a priest at a time when many priests were not well educated, whose lives were not always edifying, and who often had to please those on whom they were dependent for support (often a nobleman), to the disadvantage of the people they were called to serve. Dominic and his friars gave us a new image of priesthood, one that reflected the life of the Eternal Priest, whose mission was to proclaim the Truth received from His Father, and to offer Himself in sacrifice for His people. His kingdom was not of this world, and His authority was exercised only in the realm of spirit and truth.

Is not this the image of priesthood envisioned by the Second Vatican Council's Decrees on the *Training of Priests* and the *Ministry and Life of Priests*? They call for a focus on intellectual and moral training, a bond among priests in the exercise of their ministry, and a demand to relinquish to the laity the social and temporal responsibilities which rightfully belong to them. The priest has the mission to unite the People of God in worship and in charity, which is best fulfilled not by power but by moral persuasion with word and example. Dominic insisted on scriptural study for all his preachers, in addition to three very important components in the life of a Christ-like priest, namely, prayer, simplicity of life, and a bond of community with other priests in imitation of the Apostles. He showed the Church that these were the necessary ingredients of holiness for priests, who in union with their bishop, are called to effect the salvation of souls.

Dominic's success demonstrated that priests serve best when they share a disciplined and prayerful life in community with other priests and are not hindered by obligations which are best left to others. They must be recognized always as men who live for the Kingdom of Heaven and are not concerned with this world's power and prestige. We know that priests today are seen so often as administrators of Church properties and other temporalities, a responsibility that is often a great distraction from their spiritual mission. Also many are fully occupied in work that does not require sacred orders. It certainly seems that this situation places an obstacle in the way of the Council's hopes for today's priest. Some have wondered aloud whether there is courage anywhere to risk turning temporal responsibilities in the Church over to the laity, or at least to deacons. Until this happens, it has been expressed, true reform of the priesthood will not take place, which means the Church itself will not be renewed as the Council envisioned.

Francis and Dominic helped revitalize the Church in the 13th century by founding new forms of religious life. We might say that they met the critics half-way, by adopting the form of evangelical life which the heretics were practicing. They brought the Church to the people, not by advocating a change in her nature, but by promoting a new style of priesthood and vowed life. The evangelical life of canons and monks was not discontinued, but new ways were needed in a changing society. Priests and religious went where the people were. They did not want to be a "privileged" class in the medieval sense, but a "servant" class in the Gospel sense, according to the example of Jesus who *did not come to be served but to serve and to give His life as a ransom for many* (Mt 20:28).

Francis founded a brotherhood, which complemented Dominic's Order of Preachers. The simple life of the Friars Minor, most of whom were not priests, reflected the way Jesus lived, not in His priestly role, but in His everyday life as one of us. They were committed to work with their hands, begging for sustenance if necessary, and to go from place to place preaching "the simple word," which was more exhortatory than theological, i.e., what we must avoid and what we must do to please God. One thing the Friars Minor preached more by example than word was the respect due to priests because of their association with Jesus in the Eucharist. They were not to despise or ignore a priest, in spite of any human weakness he might display.

Since Franciscan and Dominican spirituality focus on the human nature of Jesus, as brother to us all and as priest of the new covenant, these traditions are the natural inspiration for all who are concerned with the *Up-to-date Renewal of Religious Life*. Religious are consecrated to the service of Jesus and His Church. Their refounding can be no better served than by developing closer collaboration with the diocesan clergy. The Church needs the example of support and respect for priests as those who provide us a personal and daily bond to Jesus. Francis and Dominic have shown us that the distinctive but complementary roles of priests and religious are necessary if renewal is to be effective.

Success in priestly renewal, however, may depend more on those laity who follow the example of Francis and Dominic than on religious, if for no other reason than there are more of them. They are the ones who have a continuing close relationship with the diocesan clergy. The two great works in any parish community are natural for them. Leadership responsibility in the catechetical program fits the Dominican profile. Service to social minorities and the marginalized to keep them in touch with Jesus is the work proper to those who follow Francis, just as he himself showed great compassion for lepers. By fulfilling their proper role in the Church, faithful to their own priesthood (of the laity) and in imitation of the humility of Jesus, those who live by Franciscan or Dominican spirituality and are active members of their own parish communities can promote respect for the priesthood and contribute to the clergy's own self esteem and identity.

Getting closer to our own age, we have the contribution to Church reform by Saint Teresa and Saint Ignatius. Their emergence at the very time of the Council of Trent places them in the center of the Church's call for renewal in the 16th century. Their renewed influence ought to have a great part to play today, so reminiscent of their own time. The revolt of Luther and those who followed was possible because of doctrinal ignorance among the faithful and the attitude in the emerging nations that the papacy was a foreign power. The Church's spiritual mission became eclipsed for many because of the political maneuverings in which she had become involved. Her mandate from Christ as the "all-embracing sacrament of salvation" needed a defense. This called for the formation of leaders among the clergy and laity alike. At least as important, and in a fundamental way more so, the faithful needed a greater awareness that they too are called to holiness of life, to a personal union with God. Enter Ignatius and Teresa.

The Council's Decree on the *Church's Missionary Activity* clearly makes it the responsibility of all to promote the development of Christian communities both in places where there already is a native clergy and also where the Church still depends on foreign missionaries. It might seem rather presumptuous to suggest that Ignatius and Teresa have the most to offer in this regard. Yet I remind everyone that the joint patrons of the missions are Saint Francis Xavier (a Jesuit) and Saint Thérèse of Lisieux (a cloistered Carmelite).

The admirable history of missionary activity by the followers of Ignatius is well known, as is their great success in the field of Catholic education. Many others went before them but they gave the Church a new energy and a new approach to the challenge of preaching the Gospel to all nations. The intent of Teresian spirituality is to offer the whole of one's energies for the growth and well-being of the Church, to sacrifice oneself with Jesus for the salvation of souls, which defines the spirit of missionary life. The missionary must be adventurous, and the followers of Ignatius have shown that they count no sacrifice too great for the spread of the Gospel. To balance that direction, we have Teresian spirituality which has as its root the need to abandon one's own interest and ambition to God by a separation from any personal convenience or preference. Only with this kind of generosity and spirit can missionary efforts be successful. Thus as we have seen previously, Ignatius gave a new form of religious life to the modern Church, and Teresa gave us the redemptive spirit that must animate religious life and lead us to generous service.

As if a corollary to the mission Decree, but essentially connected with it in this modern era, the Second Vatican Council has also given us Decrees on the *Apostolate of Lay People* and the *Means of Social Communication*. Both create challenges to the missionary and education elements of the Ignatian apostolic dimension. To be effective apostles, the laity need formation, and Ignatius has shown us how this is done. His followers have perfected his techniques and their imitators are legion. The Jesuits have also brought the Gospel influence to the various fields of science and technology, so we should expect them to be found at the forefront in the area of communications to be used for the promulgation of the Gospel message. Ignatius propelled into being one of the most successful educational and missionary operations in the Church's history. Indeed many of the apostolic orders and congregations of men and women that have been founded since 1556, although usually focused on more narrow apostolic aims, have adopted Ignatian spirituality in addition to Ignatian apostolic techniques. Other new foundations that had as their purpose the spiritual and corporal works of mercy often adopted Teresian spirituality in their service to Christ the Redeemer.

The proclamation of the Gospel, the apostolate of lay Catholics, and the developing area of electronic communications all become one package when we think in terms of renewal for this period of Church history. Those laity who follow the spiritual way of Ignatius should naturally be the leaders in the evangelical methods of this generation and be examples to all Catholics of what can be done by the laity in the propagation of the Faith. The laity who follow other traditions, of course, have their special dimension to add in the sanctification of the temporal order. But when we think in terms of reaching out far and wide, we need the vision of Saint Ignatius. When the focus of living the Gospel is closer to home, to serve others as the friend of Jesus, in most cases those who pursue this path of holiness find the redemptive spirituality of St. Teresa to be the most effective. Mary, the Mother of Jesus, is for them Mary the Mother of the Church, as well as Mary of Nazareth.

We believe that each tradition has a distinct apostolic profile, although their labors may overlap. Here our intention is only to suggest that the efforts by the followers of the various traditions could best serve Church renewal by being focused on their particular charisms. This would mean that Augustinian and Benedictine efforts be concentrated on the relationship of the *universal* Church to the broad society. Dominican and Franciscan influence ought to be directed within the *local* Church as it develops the Christian community, focusing on the work style of priests and religious. The Ignatian and Teresian spiritualities best serve in support of the *laity*, as they fulfill the Church's expectation for them to bring the modern world to Christ.

Renewal is everyone's work. Success depends on the generous cooperation by each area of expertise. We are one Body of Christ. Let not the hand say to the foot: "I have no need of you." No one tradition has all the answers. But each has its purpose and its own style. Each must be true to its heritage so that God may be glorified. Jesus demands it of us. The Church begs us for a faithful response.

CHAPTER EIGHT

CLOTHED IN HUMILITY

The uniqueness that each of the *Great Six* has brought to the holiness of the Church includes the contribution of their personal motivations as they sought union with the Triune God. The relationship to Jesus that each developed, plus the style of prayer that such relationship generated, as well as the form of community life in which the spirit of each was fostered, do not give us the full picture. In the pursuit of holiness there was the daily struggle to practice the virtues that governed specific actions of their lives and brought them to the perfection of charity. Sanctity implies the heroic exercise of every Christian virtue. As distinct expressions of the Incarnate Son of God in this world, each of our saints put emphasis on a different balance of the virtues. They gave a practical priority to that virtue which drove the others, and indeed encompassed them.

As intelligent human beings we do things with reason — saint or sinner. Our reasons may be selfish or altruistic, and they may not always be fully sensible even to those close to us. But from our personal perspective we find them very reasonable. For instance, people who are not satisfied with just "making a living" will often work 60-80 hours a week for any number of motives. These may be money, ambition, a sense of accomplishment, prestige, etc. They often sacrifice many other good things, such as family, leisure, health, etc., to attain a goal that to them is paramount. In reality, we often combine many reasons for doing things, but the one that keeps us going has priority and supports all the others.

Let us first reflect on the complexity of our human condition. The mixture of motivations — our weaknesses and strengths combined in the one person — makes it very difficult to know the precise reason why we do what we do, much less why others act as they do. Yet it becomes necessary to know ourselves if we are to remain faithful to Jesus. The need to be fulfilled in our person, to develop a sense of self-worth, is often frustrated as we are beset by temptations to laziness, envy, or revenge. If these sinful tendencies are not taken seriously, we undermine any efforts to respond to grace.

Then, too, discouragement often assails the beginner once the spiritual journey has begun, because we soon become aware that the road to holiness is long and arduous. And let us not forget the ever present tendency to flee monotony through self-indulgence. We rightfully look to the example of the saints for steadfastness of purpose.

The practice of virtue is the proof of holiness as well as its impetus. We state immediately that our saints are in agreement that humility has first place, and indeed is fundamental to the practice of all the virtues. It is indispensable for all who would love God, since it dissipates one's obsession with self. Love is the ultimate goal of holiness, and pride is the antithesis of love.

Augustine in the first chapter of his *Rule* warns against pride as an insidious enemy that undermines our love of God by contaminating even our good works. Benedict outlines the essence of his teaching on holiness in the twelve degrees of humility that are the steps that the monks must take in their search for God. Dominic stresses humility as the first stage in the way of prayer and the understanding of Scripture. Francis considered humility to be the "guardian and the ornament of all the virtues" (*II Cel.* #140). Ignatius in his *Exercises* speaks of the three modes of humility which set the conditions for a deepening understanding of the Scriptures and make us responsive to the force of Christ's example. Finally, Teresa in her writings constantly returns to the theme that genuine humility is the only solid foundation for the spiritual life.

Various Paths to the Humble Life

We need now to highlight the distinct manner in which each saint exercised the "practical" virtues that brought them to their humble state. Humility is a spiritual condition that everybody requires but is not attained or expressed by everyone in the same way. Hence, in each saint's uniqueness we look to find the virtue that was the focus of growth in humility. It is presumptuous, to say the least, if we place the adjective "humble" before the name of any saint, as if that virtue distinguishes him/her. Rather, the difference is the style in which the humility was attained and expressed.

Humility is so fundamental to holiness that we do not ordinarily distinguish between Augustinian humility, Benedictine humility, etc. However, all my religious life I have heard distinctions made between Franciscan obedience, Jesuit obedience, and Benedictine obedience. I suppose that others speak of Augustinian, Dominican and Carmelite obedience. Until my later years I had a good idea of Franciscan obedience in principle, but since there were monastic and Ignatian influences in my formation, the practice of Franciscan obedience was never perfectly clear to me. Only now do I realize that the "surrender of one's will" can be lived out in different ways, that there are concrete differences in the ways that our saints reached the perfection of charity.

My confusion was greatest when I reflected on the community lifestyle of different cloistered religious. They professed distinct spiritualities, but seemed to be so much alike.

Are Benedictine nuns, who truly embody the monastic tradition, different from Carmelite nuns or Poor Clares? Indeed, I wondered particularly why an apostolic order has a contemplative counterpart, e.g., cloistered Dominicans or Augustinians? It seemed to me that only the Jesuits were consistent, with no cloistered component. Now I understand differently.

I discovered the differences not so much in the externals of lifestyle (although that plays a part), but in the special way they exemplified the meek and humble Christ in the pursuit of their own sanctification and for the edification of the Church. This understanding was most helpful when I was asked how married men or women, with families, could realistically choose to follow different spirituality traditions, since the social conditions that surround marriage are often identical. In time I had learned to explain how a Secular Franciscan differed from members of other secular orders.

My explanations began with descriptions of the relationship each felt toward Jesus — as reviewed in chapter three of this book — and how each was called to live the Gospel either through special apostolic works or by a particular lifestyle. Then by concentrating on the virtue that each saint exemplified, I was able to bring the distinctiveness of the spirituality into focus. None of this makes sense, of course, unless the person of Jesus remains intact. We do not divide Him up among the saints. The *special* virtue of which we speak is the one through which and in which all other virtues are perfected.

I have sometimes phrased it this way: "In heaven there are no Franciscans; just those who, while on earth, followed Jesus in the way of Saint Francis of Assisi."

To distinguish our *Great Six* by the one virtue that most effectively separates each one from the others will require that we demonstrate how in the practice of the one virtue, they effectively practiced all of them. The ultimate object of any virtue is the perfection of charity (love) which is expressed in our relation to others by acts of generosity, kindness, respect, etc. We reach perfect charity by traveling the road of humility within a special style. The virtues on which I focus are: **obedience, trust, poverty, mortification, constancy** and **penance**.

One at a Time

We begin with Benedict, and do so because his spirituality goes directly to the fundamental purpose of our Christian life: union with God. He had separated himself from the centers of human activity in order to seek God in solitude. Eventually he became the leader of other like-minded men in the ordered life of a monastery. He readily saw that such a close association demanded a submission of each monk's will for the success of their common effort. His *Rule* lays out very detailed prescriptions to attain the purpose of monastic living. Taking the place of Jesus who alone leads us to the Father, the abbot has over-all charge of the monastic routine and all obey him in accord with the *Rule* they have vowed to God. He directs the monks in the spiritual (formation), the sacred (worship), and the mundane (work). Such complete submission of will fosters the fundamental virtue of humility, for often the person who is obeyed can display human weaknesses, and does not always direct the affairs of the monastery to everyone's liking. In effect, a monk's submission is made in service to the entire community.

Monastic obedience can be reflected in the secular world. A follower of the Benedictine tradition of spirituality who is not a monk or nun finds ample opportunity to sacrifice personal ambition or convenience to the good of the "community," e.g., family, parish, work-place, etc. The way my own father worked and prayed reflected a dedication to God, his wife and children, and his Catholic Faith that would rival the zeal of the most committed monk. Likewise, those who hold such a position of authority in family, Church, or society (*a la* the abbot), if inclined to abuse their position, need only remember that Jesus, Son of God, was Himself subject in obedience to Mary and Joseph and even unto death on a cross.

The truly **obedient** man will place complete *trust* in God whose will is expressed not only through the decisions and guidance of the human beings whom He has placed over him, but also by every circumstance that affects his life and of which God is well aware and permits to occur. The service of his community (religious or secular) calls for a spirit of *poverty* in the sharing of talents and possessions for the good of all. The difficulties of living in obedience to another provide ample opportunities to do *penance* for sins committed since obedience frequently requires attention to disagreeable tasks. An obedient life, as the *mortification* of selfish impulses, brings an ever-deepening purity of intention to the adoration of God. Obedience as a sacrifice of ambition focuses attention on the fulfillment of God's will, and away from the vagaries of personal preferences (virtue of *constancy*).

Obedience, through which we place our wills in the hands of God, is the moral expression of a faith that deepens a willingness to admit our own nothingness before our Creator and the inadequacy of our efforts apart from Him. Obedience can bring together all the virtues and places us on the sure path of humility which steadily directs the soul to union with the Triune God.

We move now to consider Teresa. She went well beyond the realm of faith to live in profound hope of receiving what God has promised, namely, eternal life for those who love Him. The realization that this promise includes work, suffering, rejection, misunderstandings, etc., demands a complete *trust* in the Father who asks us to share in the redemptive act of His Son. This is the foundation of Teresian spirituality, applicable to all.

Teresa's life, and in more recent times the life of the
Little Flower, Thérèse of Lisieux, demonstrates profoundly the
vocation to be "a victim for love." Until she was 39 years of age
Teresa was an "on-and-off" saint. She kept thinking about
developing a serious prayer life, and did give it at times a per-
functory try. However, when after fifteen years of mediocrity
she finally resolved to answer the call to holiness, she only
enjoyed a brief time of spiritual consolations and extraordinary experiences at prayer. God, so to speak, had enticed her
into His inner circle. Her decision to join some other nuns of
like mind in a more austere community began her life of total trust in the good Jesus. Through the grace of prayer she
knew that He loved her, and she was certain that He wanted
her life to go in the direction which she had undertaken. Her
move brought down the wrath of some ecclesiastical and civil
leaders. Difficulties, both from within and without the community, only multiplied when she began to establish other
foundations of her Carmelite reform.

Yet for many years she could not find comfort even in
prayer, as she had before. She found that one who serves completely must become detached not only from human consolations but from those of the spirit as well. To live only for Jesus
had become her life, even when she had no idea what her
Friend was up to. She sometimes *complained* to Him that He
could do a better job of watching out for those who were on
His side. Yet, all through the trying years she was writing her
great works of mystical theology, which were to help form the
spiritual life of those for whom she was responsible, and to
answer the questions of her spiritual directors. She depended
on them to protect her from any possible delusion in seeking
to know the will of God.

To be detached from the honors, successes, and consolations of this world and to live in the hope of eternal joy may
appear to be a very plausible, albeit difficult, goal in a cloistered life which is formed by constant prayer. However, for

one engaged daily in work, business, family life, or any other human activity the approach seems futile. Can one faithfully bear all labors, physical difficulties, and disappointments when to walk away is not a possibility? A commitment has been made to God and to those for whom we are responsible.

The answer is the same one that Teresa gave us. To keep in mind that *all things work for the good of those who love God* (Rm 8:28) is to live in "trust and self-surrender" to Him who demonstrated His love so absolutely by accepting death on a cross for us. He remains with us always, asking us to join Him in the work of redemption through a share in His suffering. This awareness makes trust under trying circumstances very possible. Trust, however, will soon disintegrate and turn to resentment unless personal prayer (intimate conversation with Jesus) is a paramount feature of daily life.

Trust in Divine Wisdom makes one ready to *obey* whenever God's will manifests itself under whatever circumstance, since we learn not to rely on our own judgment, but are ever ready to put aside our own interests for the good of others and the good of the Church. It inculcates a spirit of *poverty*, because we will be asked to share our talents and possessions with His people. Trust in God is tested by every adversity and becomes the foundation for our life of *penance* and provides *mortification* of our senses and self-interests in preparation for a life that is a continual act of offering to God our "daily works, sufferings and joys." Love, ever strengthened by trust, makes for *constancy* in doing good.

Teresian spirituality has been given new life in our generation by the influence of the "little Teresa," St. Thérèse of the Child Jesus. Her *Way of Spiritual Childhood*, total self-surrender to God's unfathomable love in every phase of our daily life with the confidence of a child, has become the strength of innumerable "little" people — those whom the world will never know, but who faithfully fulfill their daily responsibilities to family and community, and whose lives seem to be a constant prayer. My mother was one of them.

My way was to be different. I found the Jesus that Saint Francis had discovered, namely, the Son of God who became our brother and shared our humanity in all its dimensions, except sin. After leaving the comfortable circumstances of his father's house, Francis grew steadily in the spirit of prayer. He became aware of his own littleness before a wonderful Father who loved him. Responding to a genuine Fear of the Lord, his conversion began. He was drawn to those who were the "lesser ones" in the society of his day, i.e., the peasants, the lepers, etc. He did not become their advocate before the powerful, but rather he began to share with them their poverty and minority status. He understood that this is what Jesus had done from the beginning of His life with us, being born as a poor child in a stable, growing up the son of a working man, and living among the common people. Then He died on the cross in the company of thieves.

In time Francis began to exhort others to realize this great reality, that God our Father loved us so much that He sent His Son to live as we live. He did not spare Him from any difficulty in the human condition, including work and suffering. At first Francis was alone in his lifestyle, but others soon joined him. The followers of the "Little Poor Man of Assisi" became so identified with Jesus in His poverty and with the lower classes of society that even in this modern day Franciscans are expected to live as the poor and to exhibit the humility proper to those who choose to be part of a minority.

In reality, the Gospel calls all Christians to be *poor in spirit*, to recognize that everything we have and are is a gift from God that is to be received in gratitude and also be used for the good of others. This includes life itself, our wealth, time, talents, and indeed our Catholic Faith. The people who share our lives are also God's gifts and for these we must be especially grateful. But Francis did more than be grateful, and we might ask whether his imitation of the poverty of Christ is for our inspiration only, or truly for our imitation. Yet all through the ages many have wanted to follow his way exactly. Those who are faithful to the tradition of Franciscan spirituality are identified with the economic and social minority in the places where they live. This calls them to respect the rights that everyone has from God by becoming *instruments of peace* everywhere.

Yet to be poor is not a virtue, or all the poor (except those with a desire to be rich) would be saints. Poverty is a virtue only when it is lived so as to be close to the poor Christ and with those with whom He identified on earth. Hence, those who desire to live the humility of the poor together with Jesus live simple lives, without ostentation in dwellings, clothing, etc. Francis of Assisi is their model who reflects the Gospel image of Jesus Himself.

The **poverty** tradition of the Franciscan spirit influences very directly the practice of all the virtues. First of all it inculcates a need to be *obedient* to every person in the spirit of service because a poor person has no reason to feel superior to anyone. In Francis it was especially evident in his dealings with those whom Christ chose to lead the Church, namely, priests, bishops, and in particular the Pope. In his desire to bring the peace of Christ to all, Francis treated the rich and powerful, not as masters, but as brothers and sisters who have responsibilities to society. He demonstrated by his example that they too must treat everyone, low-born and well-born, with justice and compassion.

A spirit of poverty makes *trust* in Divine Providence an absolute necessity in both the spiritual and temporal order. To be anxious about the future would indicate a lack of confidence in God. Also the intentional pursuit of simplicity is in itself the practice of *penance* for prior sinful excesses and the *mortification* needed to control the desire for comfort and prestige. A man who practices simplicity in his temporal affairs will know the peace that comes from the *constancy* of love, even to the point of rejoicing to share the poverty of Christ our brother as He hung upon the cross.

At the time that Francis in Italy was directing the attention of the Christian people to the humanity of Jesus, we find Dominic in France doing the same. The intrepid Spaniard had a special apostolic mission from God, namely, to proclaim the Truth that is Jesus in a way that relates what we believe to the circumstances of everyday life. Truth is known by the mind and understood with the heart and brings us to divine love, because it dwells with the Persons who are the Triune God. The Church has the divine commission to teach all nations and all peoples, all families and all persons, everything that the Lord Jesus gave to His apostles. Dominic showed us how this is to be done. What better way than to preach as Jesus did?

In Dominic's time the official "ambassadors of Christ" were not always perceived as exemplary messengers of His teaching. The enemies of the Church exploited the ignorance of the people and turned them against the clergy and the Faith. Dominic recognized this as the basic problem in dealing with heresy. In his preaching efforts he stressed to his companions that people are open to the teachings of Christ only if those who proclaimed them showed forth a simple lifestyle imbued with prayer and charity toward all. They were to conduct themselves just as Jesus Himself did when preaching among the people. This demanded that the messenger have a knowledge of the Son of God as revealed in the Scriptures, a loyalty to the Church that is His presence in the world, and an intimate identity with Jesus as the master whose love they proclaim.

The Dominican tradition recognizes an approach that reflects the eternal Truth, i.e., Jesus as priest who brings salvation through sacrifice. For many who follow the way of Dominic this consists in a life dedicated to proclaiming the Word, but many more make Jesus known by the service of charity toward the needy in body and spirit. Any who have the responsibility to pass on the Faith, e.g., bishops, priests, deacons, catechists, parents, etc., well know that loyalty to the Master and His message requires a discipline of intellect and a strong control over the demand for physical and emotional fulfillment. Our sensual appetites focus interest on ourselves, and often lead us to take the path of least resistance when faced with challenges. Innate sinfulness, self-interest, and intellectual pride are always ready to conspire with the forces of darkness.

By following the example of Saint Dominic himself whose practice of **mortification** touched every area of his life, his followers readily understand the value of a well-ordered mind and spirit. This control over the lust of the flesh and the pride of life strengthens *obedience* to the magisterium of the Church from which comes the mandate to teach in the name of Christ. Such discipline of will inculcates within the teacher a humility which recognizes that only God's gift of faith brings anyone to the acceptance of the divine truth. Thus it generates a *trust* in the God who will arrange in His own good time the moment of conversion for those whom we teach or are called upon to edify.

The simple lifestyle that Dominic demanded of his preachers, so that their words would have power to convince the doubtful, calls all who follow Dominican spirituality to cultivate a spirit of *poverty* that is the fuel of the generous soul. It provides opportunities to live the life of priestly sacrifice, of *penance* for the remission of sins in the messenger and in those to whom he/she ministers. Finally, mortification strengthens one against the temptation to give up in the face of difficulties from without or frustrations from within. Truth is often best served by the *constancy* of one who faithfully carries the cross and offers sacrifices from "the sanctuary of the heart" where the love of the Triune God is attained through contemplation.

Now we consider the virtue that drives the "newest" spirituality tradition, that which was begun by Ignatius of Loyola over four hundred years ago. He was greatly influenced by his reading of the lives of Francis and Dominic during his recuperation from the wound that ended his military career. Yet he took from them only the inspiration of their courage to begin new adventures. His way would be unique for the time, and be amazingly successful. That success has carried down to our present day and the power of Ignatian spirituality is very much in evidence today.

Ignatius, beginning at Manresa, set out on the long road that brought him to the priesthood. At the University of Paris he inspired six other students to join him in his hope to come to the aid of the Church in her hour of turmoil. The plan he offered to Pope Paul III was so evidently the proper response to the urgent need of the day that the Company of Jesus received its mandate rather quickly. Ignatius and the hundreds who soon rallied with him brought an extraordinary intensity to the task of making the saving power of Christ known to the world. They focused their energies on education and the propagation of the Faith. His *Exercises* became the handbook, inside and outside the Society, which prepared countless numbers in a spiritual program that strengthened them for the defense of the Church.

Ignatian spirituality became fundamental to many other religious institutes that were founded in the subsequent centuries. The new apostolic congregations differed primarily in the manner in which they organized to accomplish very specific purposes. The other traditions also generated their own new forms, but it does appear that Ignatius had the broadest influence in the Catholic Reformation period. The Ignatian way was and is successful because it embodies strength. It challenges the faint-hearted and prepares its participants for great efforts in the service of the Lord. The secret of the followers of Saint Ignatius is their *constancy*. Otherwise, how explain their robust revival after the period of suppression (1773-1814)?

Ignatian spirituality is very pragmatic. The first week of the *Exercises* inculcates the awareness that we are always capable of cowardice in the face of the enemy, which is our own sinfulness. There is the daily need to reflect on this weakness (*examen*), and to resolve to fortify ourselves in view of past failures (*penance*). This theme permeates the first week of the *Exercises*. **Constancy** demands that victory over the forces of ignorance comes before personal comfort (*mortification*). It calls for the use of all resources of body, mind, and intellect (spirit of *poverty*) to extend the borders of salvation to every nation and people. This begets unquestioning *trust* in Christ to whom belongs the victory, in spite of the difficulties that service of the Lord entails. Finally, Ignatius knew that loyalty of his Company to Jesus required fearless *obedience* to His Vicar on earth and to all who guide His Church as she carries out the mandate of Christ to proclaim the Gospel everywhere.

The methods of Ignatian formation allow for no shortcuts. Training is vigorous and extensive. Any variation must not affect the basic spiritual foundation, but be concerned only with the practical needs of the work being done in a particular time or place. That is why the way of Ignatius appeals to many who are not Jesuits but who feel a call to go and get something done in the name of Jesus, to commit themselves to the service of the Church and of the world. There are also those who want to enter the fray against social injustices. They, too, know that they must be spiritually well-prepared or be over-powered by the forces of evil that are everywhere. They find that the Ignatian approach suits them very well.

Now to complete the Gospel mosaic we return to the beginning — with Augustine. He crystallized the spiritual forces of his day into a system for growth in grace. The experiences of many holy persons before him, including hermits, anchorites, monks, and nuns, were brought into focus on the ultimate goal obtained through the redemption of Christ, namely, life with the Triune God. The *Rule* he wrote was to guide those who live in community, committed by vow to the service of God and the Church.

In his youth the power of Augustine's great mind was

stifled by his uncontrolled lusts and fascination with pagan philosophy. Only when he had allowed the grace of God to take over his will was he able to harness his intellectual gifts for his own salvation and the glory of God. To keep on the course he had begun, he saw the need to be associated with others of like mind, so that even as a bishop he remained part of a community from which he obtained support and strength. From him the Church accepted the principle that religious life is essentially lived in community, secured by the vows of poverty, chastity, and obedience.

Augustine, in his writings, shares with us the wonder which he experienced through the knowledge of God's goodness. He marveled at our great destiny that had been renewed by the life, death and resurrection of His Incarnate Son. He also knew that the call to share the life of God was in constant jeopardy from our fallen nature, particularly the lust of the flesh and the pride of life. Our human life is elevated to the divine, but it remains part of the world in which we work. Daily we are called to choose between God and the evil that surrounds us.

With his own experience to guide him, Augustine wrote a *Rule* that is very pointed in prescribing the means to overcome the temptations that our inherited sinfulness opens up to us. Having laid out what is needed to live in harmony as a community and the power of prayer to the attainment of this end, he entered immediately into the need of **penance** to discipline our selfish concerns for bodily comfort and social honors.

The direct pursuit of love, to become one with the Triune God and to recognize that all others have the same destiny, is the Augustinian way. It calls for a bond of friendship with those who are also focused on the contemplation of God's holiness. Those who do not live the community life of religious must also have a bonding with others as something necessary to live fully as Christians. We are called to be responsible for the salvation of others as well as ourselves. For many the family is that community; for others it is more extensive. This sense of responsibility is particularly incumbent on those who find themselves in special positions of power. In such cases there is the ever present temptation to personal ambition and self-aggrandizement, which so often reveals itself in the abuse of authority. Intellectual pride and the weakness of our sensual nature readily stifles the conscience.

Thus Augustinian spirituality demands *constancy* in the discipline required to stay focused on higher things. To fulfill our community responsibilities is itself the *mortification* that will sharpen our spiritual faculties. *Obedience* is practiced in responding to the needs of others in community and in the respect due to the one who, as leader, has the care of the members. The *poverty* of the Gospel becomes the sharing of goods and gifts, reflecting the life of the first Christians in Jerusalem. Living together in Christian compassion with others, all of whom are beset by weaknesses even as they pursue the love of God, calls for an undisturbed *trust* in the power of God's grace to lead everyone eventually to the fullness of the supernatural life. But nothing works unless we are first committed to a spirit of conversion from our sinfulness through penance.

Treasures From the Storeroom

And so we complete the comparisons and contrasts of the *Great Six* who have given the Church such examples of sanctity. We have reviewed the differences based on historical realities and the essential components of a holy life, covering the perspective of a relationship to Jesus, an apostolic profile, and the practice of virtue. Their distinctive ways can be seen as complementary without being contradictory, and open to serve the entire People of God. We have kept our attention on their unity of purpose: to know the Father through His Incarnate Son's life, death and resurrection, within the arms of Mother Church by the sanctifying force of the Holy Spirit. Each spirituality indeed has a depth which we have not tried to reach. Enough scholars have written enough books about each of our six saints to fill many shelves in many libraries. These are available to anyone who wishes to understand a particular spirituality in greater depth. I repeat my thesis: *to understand one's own spirituality tradition well, it is imperative to know exactly how it differs from the others.* Toward this end we have kept to the essentials.

Truly, as each saint's way leads toward contemplation of God's own life, the differences between them may become less important. But their way is not. For example, reaching Rome can be a matter of traveling by plane, train, car, horseback, ship or foot. Once there the means may seem irrelevant. But while still on the way, it does make a difference.

With the enlightenment of the Spirit to inspire in us a new vision, a new perspective, we now go on to reflect on how the six traditions might direct themselves toward Church renewal in the coming generation.

CHAPTER NINE

IS THIS WHERE JESUS LIVES?

The question which heads this chapter shall be our guide as we evaluate the role of the various spirituality traditions in the call for renewal by the Church at the Second Vatican Council. The essential call was to holiness and was directed toward all: laity, bishops, priests and religious. Holiness and renewal work together. One is not possible without the other.

To illustrate, I would like to share a lesson from my early years as a priest. The memory of it helps me evaluate any situation that I find confusing or questionable. One spring afternoon as the nearby schools were letting out, I was standing in front of our friary in the Lower East Side of New York and greeting the children as they went by. One little girl, no more than eight years of age, came skipping along. She slowed down as she came near me and with eyes wide looked me over, noting my beard and habit, my Franciscan cord and sandals. I was young, about thirty years old, tall and trim. My greeting was cheerful. She had a question: "Do you live here?" "Yes, I do," I said, with a broad smile. Her next question still haunts me: "Is your name Jesus?"

Can we find a better question to ask ourselves when we enter a family home, a house of religious, a parish rectory, an institution of learning, a diocesan chancery, a nursing home, or any place where Christians gather? With the simplicity of a little child, which Jesus challenges us to become, we need to know: Is this where Jesus lives?

We must have the simple faith of children even as we face the momentous challenge that we have been given to renew the Church. No matter how difficult the current situation may be, we live on the promise of Jesus to be with us until the end of the world (Mt 28:20b). A look back on her long history bears this out. In every age and in every place spiritual giants have been raised up by God to lead His people in holiness and to show forth the presence of Jesus in the world by lives of service and suffering. Salvation in a particular generation was brought about by many who heroically shouldered the cross of Jesus to proclaim His death. We have always been blessed by the example of saints (canonized and otherwise, known and unknown, laity and religious, priests and bishops).

Historical influences and convergence are impossible to document with total accuracy, and certainly impossible to measure with complete objectivity. Much depends on the criteria employed, and those are often biased. But intelligent beings must try. Otherwise, they will plot the present course of their lives as if nothing good went before or at least that nothing from the past could have any value today.

My thesis, and I ask you to bear with me, is that the *Great Six* have set in motion distinct currents of spiritual energy, each of which began in response to a critical ecclesial situation that cried out for reform. Other holy persons have given them new emphases in view of different needs in subsequent critical times, and added their own special insights under the inspiration of the Holy Spirit. Some, it might easily be claimed, have improved on the original tradition. For very personal reasons, and prompted by divine grace, each of us has been carried by one of those currents, either in its original thrust or, more than likely, in a new configuration of purpose and motive. The spirituality that many follow often has no direct connection to any of the institutes associated with the original six, but still they live by the essential principles of one of these traditions which have become the patrimony of the Church.

Our Spiritual Legacies

In the pursuit of holiness, we each travel a path which we have learned from the Church herself, sometimes by osmosis, without always being conscious of its origin, but assured that we are firmly grounded in apostolic tradition and the Scriptures. Since the application of these spirituality traditions will pertain to everyone, we need to understand them in their historical roots but devoid of any reference to vows, community life, religious habits, cloisters, or any particular apostolic purpose. Nor can we limit ourselves to those who have vowed themselves to the service of the Church and her mission in some form of consecrated life. Seculars also have been drawn by them from their beginnings. Hence, we will also avoid defining them in a secular milieu, whether that concern the married, single, lay or cleric. We are looking for the essential ingredients in order to understand them with a universal application.

Indeed, they are not just concepts, but are given form according to concrete circumstances. A spirituality is also nourished by particular practices, beyond what is basic to the Christian life in worship and sacraments. Also there are special forms that pertain to religious life and others that are completely secular in nature. But a spirituality, to be truly a journey with Jesus, transcends the form which shapes it. Hence, we need to have a firm understanding of the six spiritual currents which are the basis of our search for renewal in this post Vatican II generation.

Augustinian spirituality is a *love* response to Jesus as a *friend* who guides us affectionately to *union* with the *Triune God.* Animated by the *prayer of wonder* at the mystery that is the divine life and strengthened by love of the *Mother of the Incarnate Word*, we pursue *Wisdom* and promote the *glory of God* in the work of the Church which unites us as God's children. This effort is supported by the discipline of *penance*, so that our human sinfulness will not impede the flow of grace.

Benedictine spirituality seeks *union* with God by an *ordered* life of *work and prayer* as a continual *act of adoration*. As *disciples* of Jesus, we show forth the *obedience* that our Master gave to His Father in all things, even unto death on the cross. By the conscientious and serene *fulfillment of our responsibilities* to God, the Church, and our families, we acknowledge before others that we have given God *priority* in our lives, though we move about in a world that draws us to its own purposes.

Dominican spirituality compels us to pursue *knowledge of the divine mysteries* by prayer and study, to understand the love of the Father who sent His Son to bring salvation to mankind, and how that work is completed by the Holy Spirit *through the Church*. With the discipline of a *mortified life* we unite with the *Eternal Priest* and strive by word and example to lead others to know Jesus our Savior, who has revealed to us eternal Truth. In this we depend greatly on *Mary the Mother of our Savior* as guide in the service of her Son.

Franciscan spirituality directs us to the amazing truth that the Son of God was born among us from the womb of a Virgin-Mother in order *to share our human condition*, to live simply and humbly among the poor, and then, taking on our sins, to suffer the injustice of a cruel death. *By imitating His style of life* and His servant-role as revealed in the Gospel, we respond to each other's needs as *brothers and sisters of Jesus* in joyful *praise* of God's goodness. We are called to remind the Church that she must always image the *poor and humble Son of God*.

Ignatian spirituality prepares us, as *companions of Jesus*, to undertake *whatever must be done* to "build up the Body of Christ." This calls for *continuing preparation* of mind and heart and spirit for *a life of service* to the ignorant, the poor, and sinners. Getting others involved *in the work of the Lord* becomes a priority. This we do in undying *loyalty* to the Spouse of Christ, guided and protected by the Virgin Mary as *Mother of the Church*.

Teresian spirituality is a *life of surrender* in total *trust* of

Jesus in whose love we rejoice. This demands unqualified service to those whose lives we share, nourished by an *intense prayer life* that seeks a union with the *redemptive mission of Jesus*. This calls for the *acceptance* of all misfortunes of body and spirit as a *privileged partnership* in the sufferings of the Cross. It demands a life of simplicity through the imitation of Mary in her home at Nazareth who as handmaiden of the Lord willingly *abandoned* herself to the will of God for our salvation.

Reform: Another Word for Conversion

Our goal is union with the Triune God through Jesus. Yet, called to baptism and redeemed from sin, we are still subject to the pull of fallen nature and struggle daily against our own basic selfishness. Even after the initial conversion from sin, there is the daily *turning away from evil and toward the Lord.* Circumstances surround us on all sides which tempt us to the easy way. The Church, as a body of redeemed sinners, has at times responded with pragmatism, rather than faith, as her history reveals from the Acts of the Apostles to these last years of the second millennium. A cursory review of our own experience will make us understand how Church leaders, even holy ones, can be unduly influenced by a society that has become dechristianized.

a. We find it easy to imagine that God is far away, especially when evil seems to be winning. There is the temptation to rely on our own energies and the power of human efforts to make life on earth bearable and productive. **Benedict** has shown us the need to "step aside" from secularist influences, and let faith govern our actions. Only when our priority is to give God the glory that He is owed will we attain the destiny that awaits us all in the Kingdom of Heaven. Church leaders have at times forgotten that in leading the world to salvation they must challenge its principles by word and example.

b. Made up of body and soul, the human being has need of material things to function, especially food, drink, clothing, and shelter. We work hard to earn the money we need. But we always want more in order to enjoy life to its fullest. And with money comes power. Yet Jesus tells us that we must *not be afraid*, that *the hairs of our head are counted*, and that God watches every *sparrow in the sky* (Mt 10:29-31). We are called to have confidence in a loving Father in heaven and to share our possessions, recognizing them as gifts from God. Any power we have ought to be used, when possible, to help the less fortunate to live a dignified human life. **Francis** has shown us how to control this constant temptation for more wealth and power. We know, too, that the Church herself finds it hard to be poor.

c. By nature we flee from pain, difficulties, confrontations. We search for pleasures and comfort, which have the power to turn us in on ourselves. The more sensual satisfaction we obtain, the more we want. The world's philosophy says: "If it gives you pleasure, do it." It goes by the name of hedonism. If we have trouble living by the words of Jesus: *Whoever does not carry his own cross and come after me cannot be my disciple* (Lk 14:27), we need the example of prayer that **Teresa** has given us. Confidence in Jesus' love will be our strength, especially when what we suffer has not been of our own choosing. Persecution is sometimes the Church's best friend.

d. As intelligent beings we always want to be right, and find it very difficult to admit our mistakes. When we become entrenched in a lifestyle or course of action that contradicts the will of God for us, we need to feel justified. We claim that what is wrong for others, and ordinarily even for ourselves, is perfectly justified in our present difficult circumstance. This denial of a constant truth, termed relativism, is the mother of heresy. **Dominic** has shown us that if our personal lives are in conformity to what has been revealed by God, we will be saved from such foolishness. When the Church's structures and practices do not reflect her belief in the Kingdom of Heaven, she is judged according to human standards even by her own children.

e. Because human beings tend to use their power to promote themselves and can be indifferent to what is happening in the lives of their neighbors, their obsession with self blinds them to the injustices that are the lot of so many of their fellow citizens. Those in positions of power focus on their own importance. They forget the words of Jesus: *What you did not do for one of these least ones, you did not do for me* (Mt 25: 45), and find themselves ignoring even the obvious needs of others, especially the poor, uneducated, sick, ill-housed, etc. **Ignatius** has called us to recognize that any injustice to a brother or sister demands our response. The Church must never sacrifice justice for security.

f. We live with the tension between our individual liberty as a child of God created for eternal glory and the need to cooperate with and support the larger society, for the benefit of all. To be so concerned about ourselves, our family, whatever is our own, that we totally ignore the needs of our neighbor, leads to society's upheaval. We will leave charity up to those who have political power. **Augustine** gave us the answer long ago, which he found in the epistles of Saint Paul. We are to be *poured out as a libation* for those whom Christ has redeemed (Ph 2:27). We are personally responsible for each other. As a communion of believers, the Church must avoid any alliance with political forces in order to fulfill her mission. Her history proves the futility of such a course.

Everyone with a serious relationship to Jesus should be able to appreciate the preceding synopsis of life's perplexities which are the constant lot of Christians. But it has particular import to lay men and lay women who, *in the midst of the world* and often surrounded by the enemies of religion, face the daily struggle to remain faithful to the Gospel of Jesus.

It Was Ever Thus

The Christian life lived in a community form had its roots in
the primitive Church as we know from the Acts of the Apostles.
From the beginning, laity and clergy alike saw the need of
spiritual support. Communities were formed for the development of life in the Spirit and for the proclamation of the Good
News of salvation to others. But for several centuries there was
nothing that would remotely resemble religious institutes as
we understand them.

The search for a deeper personal bond with God led
some to separate themselves from the concourse of human
society by fleeing to the desert. They lived in solitude, but often clustered close enough to each other to be termed a community. Saint Anthony of Egypt (251-356), a layman and the
most influential of these early hermits, was instrumental in
giving spiritual guidance to these first monks. There developed more closely-knit groups of men and women, no longer
solitaries (eremitical form) but living together in the same
dwelling (cenobitical form). The Rule(s) drawn up for them
by St. Basil the Great (329-379) set in place the predominant
form of monastic life that remains the tradition today in the
Eastern Church. Hence, religious life truly began with the
monks and nuns of the East. Saint Benedict, father of Western monasticism and a layman, seems to have been influenced
by Basil in writing his own *Rule for Monasteries.*

A case is easily made that spirituality traditions, focused
in community, began with the laity. Augustine himself, who
gave to the Western Church the vowed form we call religious
life, was part of a lay community before his ordination to the
priesthood. Subsequently the *canons,* who were formed into
communities, remained secular clergy under their bishop.
Although not a religious himself, Augustine the bishop wrote
his *Rule* for communities of men and women who were living
a consecrated life in the service of the Church. In both East

and West these lay communities of monks and nuns were formed under the aegis of the bishop to make them effective instruments of the Gospel, united to the body of the faithful.

The religious institute with centralized administration, free from the control of the diocesan bishop, is a phenomenon that emerged with the monastic reform of Cluny (10th century) but especially with the rise of the mendicant orders of the 13th century. We now had the category of "exempt" religious, subject in their internal affairs only to the Pope. In some cases, this centralization was mandated to protect such communities from suppression by bishops who were afraid of heretical groups, as well as to protect them from local political influences.

The secular orders, with papal approbation, also began as independent lay communities. The members did not live a common life (since they included those bound by marriage vows), but "came together" to share their spiritual life, support one another, and plan their joint efforts in works of charity. Unfortunately, because of political difficulties and not a few indiscretions, in time the Church placed them under the direction of the religious institutes with which they were associated. Their lay character became compromised, and they were often treated as "quasi-religious." This situation has been remedied in our time. The Second Vatican Council, having emphasized the right of the laity to found and govern their own organizations (*Apostolicam Actuositatem*, #19c), began the process by calling lay orders to be responsible for themselves, to become *secular* again.

The forms of religious life that grew from the example of the mendicants of the 13th century, whose members "went forth" in the service of the Gospel, required a spirituality that distinguished them from the double-styled tradition of canons and monks that went before. Francis and Dominic provided two very different ways of life.

But here there is a most interesting development. Because of the chaotic situation at the beginning of the 13th century, the IV Lateran Council (1215) had decreed that any new religious order had to adopt an already approved rule, which in most cases was either that of Augustine or that of Benedict. This did not apply to Francis of Assisi, since his new Gospel way had been approved by Pope Innocent III in 1209. Not so Dominic. His Order of Preachers was obliged to accept the *Rule of Saint Augustine*, modified by its own Constitutions. Dominic accepted the community life directives of Augustine as important components of religious life, but the spirituality tradition he initiated was unique to himself. So too later on, when the Church required some new religious institutes of an apostolic nature to form strong community life according to the same *Rule*, these orders or congregations did not, by that fact alone, place themselves in the Augustinian spirituality tradition.

In response to the tumult that resulted from the Protestant revolt of the sixteenth century, spiritual currents were churned up and channeled in new directions by Ignatius of Loyola and Teresa of Avila. They infused a fresh dynamism into the task of spreading the Kingdom of God and deeper insight into the pursuit of holiness. The active approach of Ignatius would lead to contemplation of the divine mysteries. Teresa's contemplative goal included a reaching out in their need to all those who have been redeemed by the blood of Jesus. From differing perspectives they brought to the Church the awareness of her need for active contemplatives. They gave a new vitality even to those spirituality traditions prominent up to that time.

New developments especially with Franciscan and Augustinian impulses were seen in Italy even before the Council of Trent. St. Angela Merici, a Franciscan tertiary, in 1535 founded the Ursulines in Brescia to teach the children of the poor, as the first non-cloistered apostolic congregation of women. St. Philip Neri in 1554 established at Rome the *Congregation of the*

Oratory in order to cultivate among the diocesan clergy a desire for holiness joined to a sense of apostolic mission. However, the convergence of all the spirituality traditions is most evident in France and Italy of the seventeenth century, developments which have had continuing effects on the Church to the present day.

Is Our Answer for Today Over 300 Years Old?

A very special and holy lady of Paris, Madame Barbe Acarie (1566-1618), drew into her inner circle of devout souls many who would lay foundations for the renewal of the Church in France. Saint Francis de Sales, celebrated Bishop of Geneva and Doctor of the Church, was one of these. Consecrated as bishop in 1603, he demonstrated to his clergy and people, like another Saint Augustine, what loyalty to Christ and His Church required. He called his clergy to theological study and holiness of life. This gentlemanly prelate reached out to the laity with a challenge to sanctity, by visiting and preaching in the country areas where the majority of the poor lived. They were ignorant of the fundamental teachings of Jesus and thus lacked a sense of a life in the Spirit. In bringing holiness within the grasp of the laity, Francis saw too the need for the Church to service the poor where they lived. With the help of a well-to-do widow, Madame Jane Frances de Chantal, he formed some women into the *Order of the Visitation* (1610) for work among the needy. Later, they were restricted to a cloistered life by the existing Church canons that governed religious women.

A diocesan priest who had been appointed by Francis de Sales as a spiritual director for the Visitation Nuns, one Vincent de Paul, had already committed himself to giving missions among the poor in the rural areas. Wherever he preached, he established confraternities of charity to respond to the needs of the people. To help his work, Vincent had formed wealthy women of Paris into groups called *Ladies of Charity* to collect money and goods for the destitute in the countryside (1617). Vincent would eventually gather the priests who were working with him into the *Congregation of the Mission* under obedience to the bishop (1625). They had one purpose, namely, to preach missions among the poor, whom the pastoral practice of the day had neglected. At this time Vincent was giving spiritual direction to a woman who was helping with the confraternities of charity, Louise de Marillac. Convinced by the signs of her sanctity, he persuaded her to form a community of women, the *Daughters of Charity*, who would give their lives in the service of the poor (1633).

The decrees of reform issued by the Council of Trent had not been promulgated in France because of a politically turbulent scene. The call for improved formation of priests through the establishment of seminaries had just not happened. Very many of the clergy were ill-trained in theology, liturgy and consequently the spiritual life. The drive to undo the damage got wide attention from the efforts of Pierre de Bérulle, a priest and later a cardinal. Beginning in 1605 he established the Oratory in many places, following the model of St. Philip Neri in Rome. By his preaching and writing he aroused the conscience of many among the wealthy to support the Church's efforts to assist their fellow citizens in faith. In time, an Oratorian named Jean Jacques Olier, convinced that more was needed than preaching to those already in Holy Orders, organized a company of priests, the *Society of St. Sulpice* (1641), for the establishment of seminaries to prepare young men spiritually and intellectually for priestly ministry. Later (1643) another disciple of Bérulle, St. John Eudes, formed his *Congregation of Jesus and Mary* which was a group of priests who would focus on holiness among the clergy. He also founded a company of *Sisters of Our Lady of Charity*, who would aid this work by prayer and sacrifice.

These communities of priests were subject to the local bishop and could not be called religious as we know the term. The women too had formed lay communities with simple vows. Today they would be called institutes of the apostolic life. Further into the century (1680) we would see a community of men dedicate themselves to the education of the children of the poor, *Brothers of the Christian Schools*, formed by St. John Baptist de la Salle.

The developments in the life of the Church in France which we have just reviewed reveal the great works that were accomplished for the glory of God and the good of His people. Since for the most part the persons involved had been educated in Jesuit colleges, we might credit the Ignatian spirit with sparking the renewal of the apostolic life in France. However, a new dimension emerged that was very different from what had preceded. Organized works of an apostolic nature, which were focused on the poor, became the foundation for new forms of consecrated life. In order to fulfill their purposes, they had to be structured very differently from those which functioned under the restrictions imposed by solemn vows. The effect of these new adventures has influenced religious life ever since.

In analyzing the currents of previously formed spirituality traditions which coursed through the apostolic life of 17th century France, we must first of all give credit for the theological foundations proposed by Francis de Sales and Pierre de Bérulle to the sainted bishop of Hippo. Augustine had focused our gaze on the person of the Son of God made Man, who through His humanity draws us into the mysterious life of the Trinity. Those in love with Jesus must of necessity be dedicated to the mission of His Church, and because of their great number and the example of Jesus must give a *preferential option for the poor.*

I cannot imagine that the spirit of Francis of Assisi was not felt, at least peripherally, through Benet of Canfield of the

Capuchins, a reform of the Friars Minor, who was so well respected in the Paris of that day. He was the confessor of Pierre de Bérulle and his writings were known to Vincent de Paul. Surprisingly too the Dominican tradition of spirituality is given only rare mention in connection with the great spiritual forces that were released in 17th century France. That is strange because in the general theological milieu, there was much emphasis being placed on Jesus as priest and victim. John Eudes and Jean Jacques Olier, himself a Third Order Dominican, gave their lives for the strengthening of the priesthood, and must have recognized that the Dominican way demanded dedication to study, mortification, and prayer as a necessary preparation for the preaching of the Gospel, which is the soul of the priestly ministry. Dominic taught us to identify with Christ the Eternal Priest in our service of His Body, the Church.

One spirituality influence that we know permeated this period is that of Teresa of Avila, beginning with Pierre de Bérulle himself. His closest spiritual confidant was Mother Madeleine de Saint Joseph, the prioress of the Carmelite convent in Paris. The Teresian influence is seen in the insistence by Bérulle that we need to commit ourselves in union with the suffering Lord Jesus to a full abandonment (*abnegation*) of our will to the demanding love of God. This reflects the total submission of Christ's humanity to His divine Person in union with the Father and Holy Spirit. Francis de Sales, Olier, and John Eudes echoed these spiritual sentiments.

Of all the currents of spirituality that coursed through the Church in 17th century France, the monastic influence is hardly recognized. Yet monasteries of monks and nuns were found throughout the country. The saints and holy persons mentioned above and in the following paragraphs had the firm belief that we are all united to Jesus as the one who most perfectly adores His Father. And the Christian life as fundamentally one of adoration is the legacy of Saint Benedict.

At the end of the century we have St. Louis Marie Grignion de Montfort taking these currents of spirituality and focusing them on the Blessed Virgin Mary as the model of our union with God through her Son. He was educated by and was always close to the sons of Ignatius. The Sulpicians of Jean Jacques Olier prepared him for the priesthood, where he absorbed the spiritual lessons of Bérulle. These were tempered by his experience as part of a group of poor seminarians, who rejoiced in sharing the poverty of Jesus. He became a Third Order Dominican and focused his ministry on giving retreats and preaching to the poor. Above all he abandoned himself totally to Jesus through servitude to Mary, and this became the hallmark of the spiritual legacy he left to the Church through the *Missionaries of the Company of Mary*, which he founded in the year 1705.

In Italy, too, special people would call for the extended apostolic life in the Church which had developed from the Council of Trent. A few of these established religious institutes that soon spread throughout the world, becoming powerful instruments in the conversion of many to a life in Christ. We have St. Paul of the Cross (1720) founding a community dedicated to the promotion of a love for Jesus Crucified, the *Congregation of the Passion*. Shortly after, several secular priests, led by St. Alphonsus Liguori, formed a company to give missions and retreats to the people, with the call to prayer and abandonment of will in union with Jesus, our Savior. They became a religious institute in due time (1732) to be known as the *Congregation of the Most Holy Redeemer*. More than a century later in 1859 a diocesan priest began a movement that would have a most profound and extensive influence in the evangelization of youth. His *Society of Saint Francis de Sales* would reach everywhere, and today the Salesians of Don Bosco is one of the largest apostolic congregations in the Church.

In highlighting the work and spiritual heritage of these saints and holy persons from the beginning of the 17th century, we do not forget that, in every generation and in almost every place, other apostolic communities of men and women were raised up for the renewal of Catholic life. They dedicated themselves to very special needs of charity and education. Many continue into our present day and are now laboring beyond the dioceses in which their work began. Also new forms of the contemplative life were established to sanctify the Church by the hidden life. Our task now, however, is to focus on our Second Vatican Council generation. What about these spiritual currents that still flow through the life of the Church? What form shall they take to be effective instruments of the new evangelization required in the twenty-first century?

We all have a personal responsibility for Church renewal whether laity, religious, or clergy. For most of us nothing more is required than a change of attitude and a spirit of obedience. Those, however, who have responsibility for others and the authority that accompanies it are required to effect the changes in the structures within which we work and/or the procedures by which we function.

First to Bethlehem and Nazareth

We look to the example of Christ in the Gospels for the attitude that is needed as the driving force of Church renewal. To that end we examine the places where Jesus can be found, beginning with His birth. Arriving without human fanfare, the stable became His first home, if only for a short time. The only ones that we know of who were invited to an audience with the new-born King of kings were the shepherds, the most humble of subjects. They would be the first to inquire: "Is this where Jesus lives?"

In Bethlehem we are immediately impressed by the powerlessness of the Son of God. No magnificence, nothing threatening. The shepherds were not intimidated by this helpless infant and His humble parents. This ability to appear welcoming was no accident. As an adult, Jesus was attractive to children, the sick, and non-Jews. He was feared only by those who felt that He was undermining their influence in the political arena and their power over the people. But to the poor and the helpless He was always a beacon of hope, reaching out to all with the peace of His Kingdom.

Is not Bethlehem a good place to begin Church renewal? Those who represent Jesus must be as approachable as the humble Son of God was to those who met Him. **Francis** of Assisi was the first to focus the attention of the Church on the humble surroundings of the birth of God's Son in the stable of Bethlehem. His special brand of Gospel poverty, identity with the poor, had proclaimed a fundamental understanding concerning the relationship of Jesus to us as a brother who did not wish to outshine the most humble of those He had come to redeem. Without minimizing His divine authority and mission, Jesus lived as one of us. Being born in poverty was the opening sign of what His life would be like.

After the sojourn in Egypt Jesus, Mary and Joseph settled in Nazareth. Their home was not a stable, nor a shanty. After all, Joseph was a carpenter. The house must have been comfortable but simple, not totally unlike those of their neighbors. Here Mary cooked meals, washed clothes, cleaned, and did everything else that a housewife and mother always has done. Joseph (and Jesus later on) worked his trade, often sweating profusely in the hot sun. When they returned home, we can hear Mary warning them not to bring any of that dirt and smell into the house. She no doubt entertained her friends and the friends of Joseph, and even the friends of Jesus as child, teenager and young adult. It is not difficult to picture someone coming to the door and asking: "Is this where Jesus lives?"

The family home of Catholics is their parish church, a house of Nazareth where the friends of Jesus gather and where people expect to find Him. Consequently, this is where the

Church must be vibrant and where we can judge the success of Church renewal. The parish is where we are formed in the Faith, where we are the People of God in worship, joining Jesus in the offering of His sacrifice and in receiving Him in the Eucharist, and where we grow in charity. In other words, the parish is our "holy" family.

The Church needs to reflect a strong presence of Jesus within the local Christian community in order to fulfill her mission. Eventually all reform must lead to a parish life where everyone may see the full message of the Gospel taught and lived because that is where Jesus unites Himself most intimately with us. In addition to vibrant worship, teaching of the faith, and charity toward all within the parish, there is need for the evangelization of the unchurched and a concern for the social issues of the larger civic community. A radical change in parish structures may well be the most serious challenge facing a bishop.

To bring the simplicity of Nazareth to the local Christian community in the planning and execution of reform, the broad outline might well be patterned on the principles which **Benedict** used to form community. The diocese would be considered as one family with one pastor, the bishop, and the priest as a disciple of the Lord and a servant of the bishop in a particular place. Everyone (cleric, lay and religious) in the house where Jesus lives enjoys equality as a son or daughter of the heavenly Father.

Throughout Galilee with Stops in Bethany

Eventually Jesus left home to begin His public life. We are acquainted with what He taught on His journeys through Galilee and Judea. The Gospels relate His miracles, and something of His association with people. We do know a little about the practical aspects of His ministry. The Gospel mentions some homes He visited, a few places He ate, and occasionally where He spent the night when He was not sleeping in a boat. During all this He traveled with His apostles. We even know that He visited Nazareth again (certainly to see His mother), as well as to attend that wedding of a family friend in Cana. This is why, just as Jesus went every place where people were, the Church must go forth from Nazareth to preach the Gospel beyond the parish community. He reminds those who would follow Him that *Foxes have dens and birds of the sky have nests, but the Son of Man has nowhere to rest His head* (Mt 8:20).

The message of salvation through Jesus has reached every corner of the world, but it has not been well received everywhere. Is this the fault of the messengers? **Dominic** thought so, and he has given us new insight into the manner of life he believed is demanded of those who preach the Gospel by word and/or example. Lifestyle and methods must conform to the divine wisdom, which is the foolishness of the Cross. The message cannot be modified to suit the convenience of the messenger. The missionary spirit of the Church to establish the Kingdom of God in every place and among all peoples is well defined in the Acts of the Apostles through the example of Saint Paul. *I have become all things to all* (1 Cor 9:19-23).

We find in the Dominican tradition the call to imitate the style of Jesus and the Apostles as they traversed Galilee in the spread of the Kingdom. In the Second Vatican Council document *Presbyterorum Ordinis* (no. 8, par. 5) we see the emphasis on the advantage to the ministry of priests when they live in community with other priests for both spiritual and moral support. This example has a commensurate effect on the faithful who witness a common effort. Such a Gospel approach becomes a constant reminder to all with a vowed apostolic commitment that Jesus is the message.

We have a pattern closer to our own time in Vincent de Paul and Louise de Marillac. They brought the Gospel to the poor by going where the poor lived and revealing to them the charity of Christ. They were willing to risk the contempt of the self-righteous who might accuse them of *eating and drinking with sinners.* The example of Jesus in Galilee was their guide.

The Gospel makes mention of the friends of Jesus in Bethany, at whose home He stopped when preaching in Judea. Mary, Martha and Lazarus must have known Him well, since He wept when He saw the sisters distraught at the death of their brother. This friendship is mentioned in John to show how the raising of Lazarus from the dead precipitated the anger of the Jewish leaders against Jesus. It brought to a head their plan to have Him put to death. But it is safe to say that Jesus had many friends, and must have been a guest in their homes also. After all, who were those special seventy-two disciples that He sent forth to the towns He was preparing to visit? St. Paul also had other friends besides his companions in the sacred ministry. His writings acknowledge those who served the churches he had established in the Gentile world. Many were women, and so we can presume that most of the others were laymen.

Evidently the early Church relied on the laity in the development of the early Christian communities, since they met in private homes. Lay men and women were the *front guard* in the age of persecution. The Church today is returning to this awareness that the laity are vital co-workers with the clergy. Together with the reform of priestly ministry the renewed apostolic commitment of the laity precisely as seculars is indispensable in our day to the fulfillment of Christ's mission of salvation to the world (*Christifideles Laici* of Pope John Paul II, 1989).

For our own day the Church could not do better than look to the example of St. John Bosco. In the nineteenth century he left us a blueprint of the cooperation possible between laity, religious, and clergy who would have distinct responsibilities as partners in the evangelization of youth. We can be hopeful that the Salesians of Don Bosco, now among the three largest institutes of the apostolic life in the Church, will show the Vatican II generation how this cooperation is possible.

In the training of laity, married or single, who are committed to the work of evangelization, the record of those who follow the Ignatian spirituality tradition is without peer. Not only the followers of **Ignatius**, but many more who have been influenced by his spirit, are very visible today in the formation of the laity. They have always been, but in the Church today their methods are needed more than ever. Some form of the *Exercises* (e.g., encounters) are being used everywhere. A process of self-discernment separates true apostles from activists. In such groupings the spirit of Bethany is paramount. The disciples of Jesus are formed by sitting at His feet, as did Mary in choosing the better part.

On Mount Tabor and Mount Olivet

Jesus is also found in two places that we can only experience in a mystical sense. The first was Tabor. Here Jesus was transfigured in glory before Peter, James and John, and the voice of His Father was heard. The other is in Gethsemane on the night before He was to suffer and die.

Tabor reminds us that Jesus is more than the man He appears to be. He is the Incarnate Son of God whose glory is hidden. So too, the Church, the presence of Jesus in this world, is not a mere human institution. She reflects the glory of the Triune God, however indistinct at times, since Jesus cannot be separated from the Father and the Holy Spirit even in His human nature. **Augustine** clarified for us the relationships within the Trinity and our personal relationship to the Triune God through the Son made Man. In this union our nature is complete and is the reason we were created. This relationship with God begins and deepens through the Church as the Body of Christ. Unless the Church's life is founded in the very mystery of God's own life, any general renewal will be temporary. We must listen for the voice of the Father.

The Church's basic nature as being one with Jesus must be recognized in the move toward renewal of her life in our day. Solutions to bring new vitality must not cloud over her life as a reflection of the Triune God, nor try to save her from the suffering inherent in her mission. United by the Holy Spirit and in praise of the Father, through the priest who acts in His name, we offer the death of Jesus again and again in the eucharistic sacrifice. The mystery of God's life must take central place in anything the Church does, because in that mystery we attain eternal glory.

The liturgy of the Eucharist as an action of the Church must be a thing of beauty and mystery in much the same way Jesus presented Himself on Tabor. In this regard we might learn from the Eastern Churches which preserve this mystery, and at the same time we will build a bridge over which the Orthodox Churches may cross to union with Peter. Also non-Catholic Christians, who decried the appearance of worldliness in the sixteenth century, should find in our other-worldliness a powerful reason to turn toward Rome.

Not long after Tabor, we find Jesus on His solemn way to Jerusalem, to go to the Upper Room and then to the Mount of Olives. As He knelt in the garden, He was overcome with fear to the sweating of blood. Judas, a friend, knew where to find Jesus, but he did not come to pray with Him. The other apostles had became too weary to *watch even one hour.* They slept. At the moment of His capture, they fled to safety for themselves. Jesus was alone to fulfill the will of His Father, the brave Peter following at a distance.

Gethsemane and Calvary remind us that His body the Church, often devoid of glory or dignity, will also suffer persecution from the forces of evil and will often join Him in His moment of sorrow. At the times when the Church is going through her Gethsemane, we must not abandon Him as did His Apostles.

This scenario should sound very familiar to us if we reflect on the troublesome times in the history of the Church. Some of the most difficult have been those reviewed in this book, and during which our *Great Six* brought to the forefront new emphases to religious life or even entirely new forms. In those days the Church's enemies often were within. Some were outright traitors like Judas, many were Church leaders who abandoned Jesus to protect their social position, and others were just fearful like Peter. Most, however, were just too tired to *watch and pray*. The Gospels relate that it was only some women and John, the youngest Apostle, who had the courage to stay with Jesus until the end. And even they, the Virgin Mary excepted, did not remember that Jesus had foretold all that would happen. The resurrection itself surprised them.

The Church needs today what she has always needed, those who *watch and pray*. She needs examples of holiness. With personal loyalty to Jesus His faithful disciples carry out the work which He assigns them, prepared to suffer even humiliation and rejection. The greater the responsibilities they have from Jesus, the closer bond they forge with Him, with special trust during trying times. With a wisdom that is inimical to this world's prudence, they are guided by the Spirit in service to the Church. This sometimes means the surrender of personal long-held preferences when renewal in the Kingdom of God demands it.

Loyal disciples are persons of prayer. But burdened by the pressure to get things done, to change ineffectual and burdensome practices in a hurry, prayer can become just part of the day rather than the spirit of the work to be done. Without prayer as the number one priority, apostles lose the motivation that gives them unfailing trust in a suffering Jesus. And love is only as strong as the trust which sustains it. This is the great lesson we have from **Teresa** of Avila, Doctor of the Mystical Life. The connection between apostolic service, Church renewal, prophetic suffering and trusting abandonment to God's will is the legacy of love from the Teresian tradition of spirituality. This spirit of excitement, from a love that is nourished in prayer, is evident in many forms of consecrated service developed since the death of Teresa (1582), not excluding the most apostolic. We are called to it again in this generation. Indeed her teaching has reached into our own time through the saint who is more and more being recognized as the epitome of a life given to the service of God and the Church, namely, St. Thérèse of Lisieux.

* * * *

I would like to end with a personal wish. My regard for the Little Flower goes back to my college days, since she was the first saint I ever compared with St. Francis. After reviewing her life for an article in my college magazine, I have always been amazed to find that, even among learned people, there is great ignorance or misunderstanding about her *little way of spiritual childhood.* A recent discovery, however, gave me a great lift. I learned that the pre-eminent Catholic social activist, Dorothy Day, looked to our young Carmelite for inspiration to keep her going when she was faced with opposition and discouragement. Bolstered by that information, I would like to suggest that the *child in their midst* whom Jesus presents to us today as the one who represents the Kingdom of Heaven is none other than St. Thérèse of Lisieux. In addition to her designation as the co-patron of the missions with St. Francis Xavier, my hope is that the Holy Father will name her the universal heavenly intercessor for Church renewal.

EPILOGUE

The spiritual life of the Church, begun at Pentecost, has flowed into various channels throughout the ages and taken shape in countless individuals and movements in every generation. The six currents we have outlined in these pages only highlight the dimensions that are possible, in response to the call of grace, to union with the Triune God and to lives of charity. To promote the Kingdom of God here on earth, we are called to rise above the human and reach to the divine. This is the mystery of the Church, which we all live in very concrete and particular circumstances.

I have spoken only about *traditions* of spirituality. There is also a place for a deeper understanding of the influence which specialized *schools* of spirituality bring to our modern times. These provide an evaluation of the theological insights and the apostolic boldness of those who responded to social conditions in previous generations. The special challenge now, however, is to rediscover the simplicity of the original sources and apply them anew to the circumstances of Church life today.

The Church has asked us once again to meet the forces that are obstructing the action of God among His people in our time. We do not need new resources, because the source of all our energy remains with us, namely, the power inherent in the death of Jesus and in the promise of His resurrection. We have the Eucharist, the very presence of Jesus, together with the other Sacraments as instruments of sanctifying grace. One problem which too often surfaces and hinders our progress in holiness is our impatience with God's ways. We are tempted to rely on human strategies to speed things up. Another obstacle is our hesitancy to develop new ways that will make incarnate God's presence among us.

The Church's basic nature was determined by Jesus, and the hierarchical structure of authority comes from Him. Yet we have many procedures that have emanated from the decisions of Church leaders or the practices of Christians themselves. These may have been Spirit-inspired, and have served well in past eras. However, they can and should be open to review and changed if they obviously dim the aura of holiness in the Church and interfere with her effectiveness as the sacrament of Christ's redemption.

I would hope that those who have read these pages and have the appropriate authority will make the bold moves necessary to effect renewal within their own domains. The goal is the conversion and holiness of clergy and faithful so that the presence of Jesus will be made manifest to our generation. My intention is to help set a parameter for renewal, so that reform might be guided by the spirituality traditions that have been so effective during past periods of turmoil. If the level of holiness is not raised within ourselves and within the Church herself, all efforts are in vain. Then we are just *a sounding gong or a clashing cymbal* (2 Cor 13:1-3).

I would like to close this contribution to dialogue with some discussion-starters. My claim of expertise in proposing them comes not only from my life experience as a parish priest and spiritual director, but especially as a missionary in the hills of Honduras, Central America. There I learned just how possible it is for the laity *to run the Church.*

In any mountain town the people saw a priest only once a month, and in any village only once a year. Yet Christian communities with their own church or chapel thrived in each place, with the same levels of sanctity and mediocrity that are found in any parish in the United States or elsewhere. We relied on lay leaders (trained in formation centers) to catechize children, instruct adults as baptismal sponsors and prepare couples for marriage. Everything in a particular place was coordinated by a trained Delegate of the Word (*Delegado de La Palabra*) who also conducted a para-liturgical service on Sundays when no priest was available. We Capuchins lived community life at a central mission station, from which we went forth to be welcomed in the towns and villages as *priests*. It was wonderful not to have the temporal administration of anything, except to maintain a jeep for travel. Where a jeep could not go, the people provided the temporary loan of a mule.

Hence, I will now dare to suggest some scenarios for the consideration of the adventurous among you. They all have practical implications that others will have to address. Yet they are worth considering on principle. They involve the structure of parishes, consecrated life in the service of the Church, and the distinct role of the laity in this age.

Pertaining to diocesan life:

a. Parishes administered by full-time deacons who live in the parish house with their families and are responsible for the catechetical program for children and adults, and the preparation for the sacraments, including the celebration of baptism and marriage.

b. Priests of the diocese, living community style in a central place, responsible to serve a particular cluster of churches.

Pertaining to consecrated life:

c. Communities of *priests* with private vows formed to serve the entire diocese in special work at the direction of the bishop.

d. Communities of *lay men or women* with private vows formed to serve the diocese in specialized needs of charity or education.

Note that both (c) and (d) describe the original form of many religious congregations.

e. Communities of *lay men or women* with private vows formed to serve an individual parish.

f. Religious communities of men or women available to be a presence in any diocese at the invitation of the bishop in order to carry on their particular purpose without a connection to any part of the diocesan structure.

Pertaining to the laity:

g. Lay men and lay women appointed by the bishop to be responsible directly to him for the temporal administration of the diocese or individual parishes.

h. The recognition among clergy and religious that the laity are not just associates with special talents and expertise, but independent partners with their own areas of apostolic responsibility.

* * * *

My book is now finished and my promise fulfilled. I can continue with the task of becoming holy, so frequently off course since I first vowed my life to the service of God and the Church. Concentration on my work sometimes overshadowed the principle that faithfulness to Jesus is more important than success. Age has given me a modicum of wisdom.

By the grace and mercy of God, I have learned that spirituality is not defined by what we do, but by our relationship to Jesus. The needs of God's people, my own capabilities, and obedience will determine where and how I contribute to the Kingdom of God. I understood in time how Francis related to Jesus as his *Brother*, a way so different from Augustine (*Son of God*), Benedict (*Master*), Dominic (*Savior*), Ignatius (*Lord*), and Teresa (*Redeemer*). These are all permanent relationships. Jesus is no longer the preacher or the miracle-worker.

The Church too must be seen as Jesus. Her success is measured, not by how much respect she gets, but by how much holiness she fosters. This also goes for religious communities and societies of the apostolic life, for history amply proves that only saints have been fully effective instruments of renewal.

APPENDIX

This is an incomplete listing of religious orders and congregations drawn up according to the spirituality traditions compared in this book. A simple questionnaire was sent to the provincial superiors of those institutes that are located in the United States. The most important question was: *Of which spirituality tradition is your institute representative?* Not everyone responded and not all institutes laid claim to any of the spirituality traditions of which this book treats. Those whose very name reveals their tradition were for the most part not surveyed.

The Eastern Spirituality Tradition

We must recognize that all spirituality began where the Church began, in the East. The rich heritage of the Eastern Churches is certainly the foundation for both the Augustinian and Benedictine traditions in the Western Church.

4th cent. - **Sisters of St. Basil the Great**, *St. Macrina* in Cappadocia, Asia Minor
1911 - Ukrainian, *Mother Helena Langevich* in Fox Chase Manor, PA
1921 - Ruthenian, *Mother Macrina Melnychuk* in Uniontown, PA

The Augustinian Spirituality Tradition

The *Rule of St. Augustine* was originally developed for men and women who had already formed themselves into communities. Augustine himself lived with a community of clerics, but he did not found any group that exists today. In time his *Rule* was adopted by clerics or hermits who wished to live a common life. The Church herself has on occasion required newly formed apostolic institutes to use his *Rule* as the basis for their community life. Also other congregations were formed according to the Augustinian spirit without using the *Rule* as written.

1120 - **Premonstratensians**, *St. Norbert of Xanten* in Prémontré, France

1210 - **Canons Regular of the Order of the Holy Cross**, *Theodore De Celles* in Huy, Belgium

1218 - **Order of Our Lady of Mercy**, *St. Peter Nolasco* in Barcelona, Spain

1233 - **Order of Servants of Mary**, *Seven Holy Founders* in Monte Senario, Italy

1298 - **Sisters, Servants of Mary**, *St. Juliana Falconieri* in Florence, Italy (1912) *Mary Alphonse Bradley* and *Boniface Efferenn, OSM* in Ladysmith, WI

13th cent. - **Alexian Brothers**, *Group of laymen* in the Rhineland and Lowlands

1535 - **Ursuline Sisters**, *St. Angela Merici* in Brescia, Italy

1610 - **Sisters of the Visitation**, *St. Francis de Sales* and *St. Jane Frances de Chantal* in Annecy, France

1625 - **Sisters of the Incarnate Word and Blessed Sacrament**, *Ven. Jeanne Chezard de Matel* in Roanne, Lyons, France

1762 - **Congregation of Divine Providence** (of Kentucky), *Bl. Jean-Martin Moye* in Lorraine, France

1807 - **Sisters of St. Joseph of Cluny**, *Anne Marie Javouhey* in Cluny, France

1807 - **Congregation of St. Brigid**, *Daniel Delany* in Tullow, Ireland

1833 - **School Sisters of Notre Dame**, *Theresa Gerhardinger* in Neunburg Vorm Wald, Germany

1845 - **Sisters of Charity of Ottawa**, *Elisabeth Bruyere* in Ottawa, Canada

1850 - **Augustinians of the Assumption**, *Emmanuel d'Alzon* in Nimes, France

1851 - **Sisters of the Most Holy Sacrament**, *Joseph Aloysius Faller* in Bellemagny, France

1851 - **Sisters, Servants of Mary, Ministers to the Sick,** *St. Soledad Torres* in Madrid, Spain

1851 - **Congregation of Divine Providence,** *Bp. William E. Von Ketteler* in Mainz, Germany

1865 - **Little Sisters of the Assumption,** *Stephen Pernet* in Paris, France

1868 - **Daughters of Divine Charity,** *Franciska Lechner* in Vienna, Austria

1869 - **Sisters of Charity of the Incarnate Word,** *Claude Marie Dubuis* in San Antonio, TX

1875 - **Sisters of the Holy Family of Nazareth,** *Bl. Mary of Jesus the Good Shepherd* in Poland

1886 - **Sisters of the Divine Compassion,** *Caroline Dannat Starr* and *Msgr. Thomas S. Preston* in New York, NY

1893 - **Sisters of the Holy Spirit and Mary Immaculate,** *Margaret Healy-Murphy* in San Antonio, TX

1911 - **Sisters of St. Rita,** *Hugolin Dach* in Wurzburg, Germany

1921 - **Grey Nuns of the Sacred Heart** in Buffalo, NY (*Marguerite d'Youville*, Montreal, 1737)

1951 - **Little Brothers of the Good Shepherd,** *Mathias Barrett* in Albuquerque, NM

The Benedictine Spirituality Tradition

Monasticism in the West has developed many forms since the time of Benedict, including the Camaldolese, Cistercians, Trappists, etc. All fall within the Benedictine tradition. It is not necessary, however, to be a monk or nun in order to follow Benedictine spirituality, as for instance:

1800 - **Congregation of the Sacred Hearts of Jesus and Mary,** *Joseph Francis Coudrin* and *Henriette Aymer de la Cevalerie* in Potiers, France

1807 - **Brothers of Charity,** *Peter Joseph Triest* in Ghent, Belgium

1829 - **Oblate Sisters of Providence,** *Mary Elizabeth Lange* in Baltimore, MD

1834 - **Adorers of the Blood of Christ**, *Bl. Maria de Mattias* in
        Acuto, Italy
1856 - **Congregation of the Blessed Sacrament**, *St. Peter Julian*
        Eymard in Paris, France
1909 - **Mariannhill Mission Society**, *Francis Pfanner* in South Africa
1923 - **Sisters of Social Service**, *Margaret Slachta* in Budapest,
        Hungary
1937 - **Medical Missionaries of Mary**, *Mary Martin* in Nigeria,
        Africa

The Dominican Spirituality Tradition

The Dominican tradition as an apostolic spirituality includes any and all work that is pursued in union with Jesus
our Priest and Savior, from mission activity to works of education and charity. The many institutes in this tradition use the
designation *Dominican* in their title.

The Franciscan Spirituality Tradition

Numerous institutes are connected to St. Francis himself,
by reason of his direct founding of three distinct orders for
men religious, women religious and laity, as well as several
reforms of the parent groups which eventually became separate entities. Many congregations of later origin have no relation to the Franciscan Order itself. Their purposes are pursued with the spirit of Francis, who taught us that we are brothers and sisters to each other as Jesus is brother to us, and we
therefore have a special responsibility to share the condition
of the poor and marginalized in our society.

1849 - **Franciscan Sisters of Perpetual Adoration**, *Six tertiaries* from
        Ettenbeuren, Bavaria
1852 - **Sisters of Mercy of the Holy Cross**, *Bl. Maria Theresa Scherer*
        and *Theodosius Florentini, OFM Cap.*, in Switzerland

1855 - **Congregation of the Sisters of Saint Felix of Cantalice**, *Bl.*
Mary Angela Truszkowska in Warsaw, Poland
1857 - **Brothers of the Poor of St. Francis**, *John Philip Hoever* in
Aachen, Germany
1872 - **Franciscan Sisters of Mary**, *Odilia Berger* in St. Louis, MO
1886 - **Servants of Charity**, *Bl. Louis Guanella* in Como, Italy
1910 - **Missionary Sisters of the Immaculate Conception of the
Mother of God**, *Elisabeth Tombrock* and *Bp. Amandeus
Bahlmann, OFM*, in Santarem, Pará, Brazil
1975 - **Servants of Jesus**, *Gene Rakoczy* in Michigan
1976 - **Sisters of Our Lady of Guadalupe and St. Joseph**, *Magda L.
García* in Gallup, NM

The Ignatian Spirituality Tradition

The *Spiritual Exercises* of St. Ignatius has inspired the foundation of numerous institutes of the apostolic life which are
not linked to the Jesuits themselves. The Ignatian tradition has
propelled into the life of the Church a spirit of missionary,
educational and charitable activity that has never subsided,
giving concrete evidence of the Christian life as one of active
contemplation.

1582 - **Order of St. Camillus, Servants of the Sick**, *St. Camillus de
Lellis* in Rome, Italy
1609 - **Institute of the Blessed Virgin Mary**, *Mary Ward* in St.
Omer, Belgium
1650 - **Congregation of the Sisters of St. Joseph**, *John Pierre
Médaille, S.J.* in LePuy, France
1673 - **Congregation of Marian Clerics of the Immaculate Conception BVM** (renewed in 1910), *Ven. Stanislaus Papczynski* in
Marian Forest, Poland
1685 - **Religious Venerini Sisters**, *Bl. Rosa Venerini* in Viterbo, Italy
1790 - **The Daughters of the Heart of Mary**, *Marie Adelaide DeCice*
and *Pierre Joseph DeCloriviere, S.J.* in Paris, France
1816 - **Stigmatine Fathers and Brothers**, *St. Gaspar Bertoni* in
Verona, Italy

1816 - **Society of Mary**, *Jean Claude Colin* in Lyons, France
1817 - **Brothers of Christian Instruction**, *Gabriel Deshaies* and *John Mary de la Mennais* in Ploermel, France
1820 - **Sisters, Faithful Companions of Jesus**, *Marie Madeleine D'Houet* in Paris, France
1822 - **Congregation of St. Basil**, *Ten Diocesan Priests* in Annonay, France
1826 - **Oblates of the Virgin Mary**, *Ven. Pio Bruno Lanteri* in Turin, Italy
1826 - **Religious of the Cenacle**, *St. Thérèse Couderc* and *John Stephen Terme* in La Louvesc, France
1828 - **Institute of Charity**, *Antonio Rosmini* in Domodossola, Italy
1833 - **Sisters of Charity of the Blessed Virgin Mary**, *Mary Frances Clarke* and *Terence J. Donaghoe* in Philadelphia, PA
1834 - **Sisters of Saint Dorothy**, *St. Paul Frassinetti* in Genoa, Italy
1839 - **Xaverian Brothers**, *Theodore James Ryken* in Bruges, Belgium
1845 - **Missionary Sisters of the Society of Mary**, *Françoise Perroton* and ten pioneer women in France
1846 - **Society of the Holy Child Jesus**, *Cornelia Connelly* in England
1849 - **Sisters of Christian Charity - Daughters of the BVM of the Immaculate Conception**, *Pauline von Mallinckrodt* in Paderborn, Germany
1849 - **Religious of the Sacred Heart of Mary**, *Ven. Jean Gailhac* in Béziers, France
1849 - **Sons of the Immaculate Heart of the Blessed Virgin Mary**, _ *St. Anthony M. Claret* in Vich, Spain
1850 - **Servants of the Immaculate Heart of Mary**, *Marie-Josephte Fitzbach* in Quebec, Canada
1856 - **Helpers of the Holy Souls**, *Bl. Mary of Providence* in Paris, France
1867 - **Comboni Missionaries of the Heart of Jesus**, *Daniel Comboni* in Verona, Italy / Cairo, Egypt
1868 - **Missionaries of Africa**, *Cardinal Lavigerie* in Algeria, Africa
1869 - **Missionary Sisters of Our Lady of Africa**, *Cardinal Lavigerie* in Algeria, Africa
1873 - **Congregation of St. Joseph**, *St. Leonard Murialdo* in Turin, Italy

1877 - **Handmaids of the Sacred Heart of Jesus**, *St. Raphaela Mary Porras* in Spain

1894 - **Missionary Sisters of St. Peter Claver**, *Mary Theresa Ledochowska* in Austria

1895 - **St. Francis Xavier Foreign Mission Society**, *Bl. Guido M. Conforti* in Parma, Italy

1900 - **Missionary Sisters of the Sacred Heart of Jesus**, *Hubert Linckens* in Westphalia, Germany

1901 - **Consolata Missionaries**, *Bl. Joseph Allamano* in Turin, Italy

1910 - **Sisters of Our Lady of Christian Doctrine**, *Marion L. Gurney* in New York, NY

1911 - **Catholic Foreign Mission Society of America**, *James A. Walsh* and *Thomas F. Price* in Hawthorne, NY

1934 - **Mercedarian Missionaries of Berriz**, *Margarita Lopez de Naturana* in Vizcaya, Spain

1941 - **Home Mission Sisters of America**, *William Howard Bishop* in Cincinnati, OH

1952 - **Sons of Mary, Health of the Sick**, *Edward F. Garesché, S.J.*, in Boston, MA

1984 - **Institute of the Incarnate Word**, *Carlos Buela* in San Rafael, Argentina

The Teresian Spirituality Tradition

To serve as partners of Jesus in His mission of redemption, as victims of love in total abandonment to the Holy Spirit in service of the Church, as taught by Teresa of Avila, is the inspiration of many apostolic communities who are not associated with the Carmelite Order.

1732 - **Congregation of the Most Holy Redeemer**, *St. Alphonsus Liguori* in Naples, Italy

1845 - **Sisters, Servants of the Immaculate Heart of Mary**, *Theresa Maxis Duchemin* and *Louis Florent Gillet, C.SS.R.*, in Monroe, MI

1894 - **Oblate Sisters of the Sacred Heart of Jesus**, *Teresa Casini* in Grottaferrata, Italy

1917 - **Carmelite Sisters of St. Thérèse of the Infant Jesus**, *Edward Soler, OCD*, in Bentley, OK
1947 - **Congregation of the Servants of the Paraclete**, *Gerald Fitzgerald* in Jemez Springs, NM
1966 - **Society of Our Mother of Peace**, *Placid Guste* in Oklahoma City, OK

The Spirituality Traditions of the Modern Era

The 17th century, especially in France, introduced new forms of vowed community life which gave a very different face to the apostolic service of men and women in the Church. They were geared toward a more active involvement in the daily lives of God's people during very difficult periods of social and political upheaval. With special emphases and differing combinations of the inherited traditions, each became a unique contribution to the Church's heritage. Their special styles continue to be very important in our own generation. Since it is difficult to separate the converging currents of spirituality that influenced the founders of these congregations, we list them in their own category.

1625 - **Congregation of the Mission**, *St. Vincent de Paul* in Paris, France
1633 - **Daughters of Charity of St. Vincent de Paul**, *St. Louise de Marillac* in Paris, France
1640 - **Daughters of the Cross**, *Marie L'Hullier de Villeneuve* in Paris, France
1641 - **Society of St. Sulpice**, *Jean Jacque Olier* in Paris, France
1643 - **Congregation of Jesus and Mary**, *St. John Eudes* in Caen, France
1680 - **Brothers of the Christian Schools**, *St. John Baptist de la Salle* in Rheims, France
1692 - **Pontifical Institute of the Religious Teachers Filippini**, *Card. Mark Anthony Barbarigo* and *St. Lucy Filippini* in Montefiascone, Italy

1705 - **Missionaries of the Company of Mary**, *St. Louis Marie de Montfort* in Western France

1737 - **Sisters of Charity of Montreal 'Grey Nuns'**, *Marguerite d'Youville* in Montreal, Canada

1799 - **Sisters of Charity of St. Joan Antida**, *St. Jeanne Antide Thouret* in Besançon, France

1803 - **Sisters of Charity of St. Louis**, *Marie-Louise Elizabeth Mole* in Vannes, France

1807 - **Sisters of St. Chretienne**, *Madame de Méjanès* in Metz, France

1809 - **Sisters of Charity of St. Vincent de Paul of New York**, *St. Elizabeth Ann Seton* in Emmitsburg, MD

1812 - **Sisters of Charity of Nazareth**, *Catherine Spalding* in Kentucky

1815 - **Society of the Precious Blood**, *St. Gaspar del Bufalo* in Giano (Umbria), Italy

1816 - **Oblates of Mary Immaculate**, *St. Eugene de Mazenod* in Aix-en-Provence, France

1816 - **Daughters of Mary Immaculate**, *Adele de Bate de Trenquelleon* and *William Joseph Chaminade* in Agen, France

1817 - **Society of Mary**, *William Joseph Chaminade* in Bordeaux, France

1817 - **Marist Brothers of the Schools**, *Bl. Marcellin Champagnat* in La Valla, France

1823 - **Daughters of the Charity of the Sacred Heart of Jesus**, *Jean Marie Catroux* and *Rose Giet* in La Salle-de-Vihiers, France

1826 - **Sisters of the Holy Union**, *Jean Baptist Debrabant* in Douai, France

1829 - **Sisters of Charity of Our Lady of Mercy**, *John England* in Charleston, SC

1831 - **Institute of the Sisters of Mercy of the Americas**, *Catherine McAuley* in Dublin, Ireland

1835 - **Sisters of the Good Shepherd**, *St. Mary Euphrasia Pelletier* in Angers, France

1837 - **Congregation of Holy Cross**, *Basile-Antoine Moreau* in Le Mans, France

1839 - **Little Sisters of the Poor**, *Bl. Jeanne Jugan* in Brittany, France

1841 - **Marianites of Holy Cross / Sisters of the Holy Cross / Sisters of Holy Cross**, *Basile-Antoine Moreau* in Le Mans, France

1843 - **Society of St. Edmund**, *John Baptist Muard* in Pontigny, France

1851 - **Poor Handmaids of Jesus Christ**, *Mary Katherine Kasper* in Dernbach, Germany

1851 - **Sisters of Charity of St. Augustine** in Cleveland, OH

1852 - **Missionaries of Our Lady of La Salette**, *Bp. Philibert de Bruillard* in Grenoble, France

1854 - **Missionaries of the Sacred Heart**, *Jules Chevalier* in Issoudun, France

1854 - **Sisters of the Humility of Mary**, *Marie Antoinette Potier* and *John Joseph Begel* in Dommartin-sous-Amance, France

1856 - **Sisters of the Holy Faith**, *Margaret Aylward* and *John Gowan, C.M.*, in Ireland

1858 - **Sisters of Charity of Leavenworth**, *Mother Xavier Ross* in Leavenworth, KS

1859 - **Salesians of Don Bosco**, *St. John Bosco* in Turin, Italy

1860 - **Servants of the Holy Heart of Mary**, *Francis Delaplace* and *Marie Moisan* in Paris, France

1872 - **Daughters of Mary Help of Christians**, *St. John Bosco* in Mornese (Piedmont), Italy

1875 - **Oblates of St. Francis de Sales**, *Louis Brisson* in Troyes, France

1878 - **Oblates of St. Joseph**, *Bl. Joseph Marello* in Asti (Piedmont), Italy

1881 - **Society of the Divine Savior**, *Francis Jordan* in Rome, Italy

1888 - **Sisters of the Divine Savior**, *Francis Jordan* and *Bl. Mary of the Apostles* in Tivoli, Italy

1892 - **Sisters of Providence of Holyoke**, *Mother Mary of Providence Horan* in Holyoke, MA

1902 - **Vincentian Sisters of Charity**, *Mother Emerentiana Handlovits* in Braddock, PA

1928 - **Vincentian Sisters of Charity**, *Mother M. John Berchmans* in Bedford, OH

Varied Spiritualities

These communities listed here claim a spirituality tradition different from any of the above. The parenthesis beneath a name indicates the spirituality of the institute.

1198 - **The Order of the Holy Trinity**, *St. John de Matha* in Cerfroid, France (*Ordo canonicus*, scripturally based, apostolate inspired by works of mercy and the life of the Trinity)

1533 - **Clerics Regular of Saint Paul**, *St. Anthony Mary Zacaria* in Milan, Italy (Pauline Charism, Renaissance Evangelism, Christian Humanism)

1554 - **Congregation of the Oratory**, *St. Philip Neri* in Rome, Italy (Lay centered built on Scripture)

1621 - **Piarist Fathers**, *St. Joseph Calasanz* in Rome, Italy (Pedagogical / Educational)

1703 - **Congregation of the Holy Ghost**, *Claude Francis Poullart des Places* in Paris, France (Openness to the Spirit)

1720 - **Congregation of the Passion**, *St. Paul of the Cross* in Italy (Unique to St. Paul of the Cross)

1812 - **Sisters of Loretto at the Foot of the Cross**, *Charles Nirinckx* in Loretto, KY (American Missionary - something from all the *Great Six*)

1821 - **Brothers of the Sacred Heart**, *André Coindre* in Lyons, France (Ignatius / Augustine / Evolved theology of the Sacred Heart)

1826 - **Carmelite Sisters of Charity**, *Joaquina de Vedruna* in Barcelona, Spain (Also Franciscan in part)

1834 - **Sisters of the Precious Blood**, *Maria Anna Brunner* and *Francis de Sales Brunner* in Switzerland (Precious Blood from Gaspar del Bufalo, Rome, Italy)

1838 - **Pallottine Missionary Sisters**, *St. Vincent Pallotti* in Rome, Italy (Apostolic - missionary)

1845 - **Sisters of the Most Precious Blood**, *Theresa Weber* in Steinerberg, Switzerland (Precious Blood)

1858 - **Congregation of the Sisters of St. Agnes**, *Caspar Rehrl* in Barton, WI (Francis / Augustine / American missionary)

1875 - **Society of the Divine Word**, *Bl. Arnold Janssen* in Steyl, Holland (Trinitarian with monastic and Ignatian features)

1878 - **Sisters of St. John the Baptist**, *Alfonso M. Fusco* in Angri, Italy (Augustine / Benedict)

1884 - **Sisters of St. Joseph of Peace**, *Margaret Anna Cusack* in Nottingham, England (Franciscan / biblical / pursuit of justice with the gift of peace)

1886 - **Sisters of St. Mary of Oregon**, *Archbishop Gross* in Sublimity, OR (Benedictine / Ignatian / Redemptorist)

1887 - **The Missionaries of St. Charles**, *John Baptist Scalabrini* in Piacenza, Italy (St. Charles Borromeo)

1887 - **Daughters of Divine Zeal**, *Bl. Hannibal Maria DiFrancia* (Rogationist - "Pray to the Lord of the harvest" ... Mt 9:38)

1894 - **Apostles of the Sacred Heart**, *Clelia Merloni* in Viareggio, Italy (Augustine / Ignatius)

1912 - **Maryknoll Sisters of Saint Dominic**, *Mary Joseph Rogers* in Hawthorne, NY (Missionary - Dominic / Teresa)

1914 - **Society of St. Paul**, *Ven. James Alberione* in Alba, Italy (Paul / Ignatius - Modern means of communication)

1915 - **Daughters of St. Paul**, *Ven. James Alberione* in Alba, Italy (Paul / Ignatius - Modern means of communication)

1922 - **Our Lady of Victory Missionary Sisters**, *John Joseph Sigstein* in Santa Fe, NM (Marian)

1924 - **Sister Disciples of the Divine Master**, *Ven. James Alberione* in Alba, Italy (Eucharistic devotion, liturgical apostolate, service to the priesthood)

1930 - **Missionary Catechists of Divine Providence**, *Benitia Vermeersch* in Houston, TX (Providence / Our Lady of Guadalupe)

1949 - **Sisters, Home Visitors of Mary**, *Mary Schutz* in Detroit, MI (Gospel / Church)

1953 - **Handmaids of Mary Immaculate**, *Mother Mary Stanislaus* in Helena, MT (Marian - Eucharistic according to St. Louis Mary de Montfort)

1953 - **Congregation of the Mother Coredemptrix**, *Dominic Tran Dinh Thu* in Bui Chu, Vietnam (Combination of several traditions)

1974 - **Little Sisters of Jesus and Mary**, *Mary Elizabeth Gintling* in Baltimore, MD (Charles de Foucauld)